THE EVERYTHING KIDS' STATES BOOK

Wind your way across our great nation

Brian Thornton

Adams Media

New York   London   Toronto   Sydney   New Delhi

Dedication

For my parents, Hal and Berniece Thornton, who fostered in me a life-long love of learning.

Acknowledgments

I'd like to thank the crew at Adams Media, especially acquisitions editors Kerry Smith and Paula Munier and editorial wunderkind Kate Powers. Also, thanks to my family and my friends (AKA my other family) at Meridian Middle School in Kent, Washington, for your support, and for making it a joy to go to work each day.

Adams Media
An Imprint of Simon & Schuster, Inc.
57 Littlefield Street
Avon, Massachusetts 02322

An Everything® Series Book.
Everything® and everything.com® are registered trademarks of Simon & Schuster, Inc.

ADAMS MEDIA and colophon are trademarks of Simon and Schuster.

For information about special discounts for bulk purchases, please contact Simon & Schuster Special Sales at 1-866-506-1949 or business@simonandschuster.com.

The Simon & Schuster Speakers Bureau can bring authors to your live event. For more information or to book an event contact the Simon & Schuster Speakers Bureau at 1-866-248-3049 or visit our website at www.simonspeakers.com.

Interior illustrations by Kurt Dolber.
Puzzles by Beth L Blair.

Manufactured in the United States of America

Printed by LSC Communications, Harrisonburg, VA, U.S.A.

10   9   8   7   6   5

ISBN 978-1-59869-263-1

See the entire Everything® series at *www.everything.com.*

CONTENTS

INTRODUCTION

The United States is a remarkable country, and we as Americans are lucky to live here. Have you ever wondered what this country is like? Maybe you know a bit about where you live, your hometown, maybe your home state, but there are fifty states in the United States. How much do you know about them?

Were you aware that the state of Alaska would fill up one-fifth of the total area of the rest of the United States all by itself? Were you aware that Hawaii has a state fish? Or that Massachusetts has a lake within its borders that has the longest name of any body of water in the whole United States? It's true!

If you're curious about your country and would like to learn more about what it is like, "from sea to shining sea," then *The Everything Kids' States Book* is intended for you. If you want to know what there is to see and do if you visit other states in the Union, if you're curious about each state's history, if you'd like to know what kinds of things are made and sold in these states, if you'd like to know wacky and little-known facts about each state, then this is the book you've been looking for!

Beginning with New England in Chapter 1 and ending with the Pacific Northwest in Chapter 10, this book sweeps across the nation we call home, telling us a bit about where we live, what we do for fun, and what our future looks like. Mixed in are tidbits such as Fast Facts, Words to Know, and Try This, all intended to keep you focused on the fun side of learning about America.

May God bless her!

he states that make up the region we know as New England include some of the oldest states in the union. For example, Massachusetts was founded as a colony nearly 400 years ago. The American Revolution started in New England, as did the American anti-slavery movement nearly a century later.

New England has supplied our country with a number of its leaders—revolutionary leaders like Samuel Adams and his cousin John Adams and John's remarkable wife, Abigail, for example. John Adams later became our second president. His son, John Quincy Adams, was also president. In the 1960s, Massachusetts senator and war hero John Fitzgerald Kennedy became the thirty-fifth president.

New England is famous for its seasons, especially for autumn, when the leaves in its huge forests turn different colors. People from all over the world come to New England in the fall to witness the changing of the leaves. A delicious effect of the seasonal changes in New England's forests is the maple syrup industry!

ALL ABOUT Massachusetts

CAPITAL: Boston

LARGEST CITY: Boston

POPULATION: 6,349,097 (2000 Census)

STATE BIRD: Chickadee

STATE TREE: American Elm

STATE FLOWER: Mayflower

STATE MOTTO: "*Ense Petit Placidam Sub Libertate Quietem* (By the Sword We Seek Peace, but Peace Only under Liberty)"

STATEHOOD: February 6, 1788

POSTAL ABBREVIATION: MA

MASSACHUSETTS: The Bay State
Geography and Industry

Massachusetts is both one of the smallest states and one of the most thickly populated states. Most of the people who live in Massachusetts live in the eastern part of the state, near the coast. The western part of the state has more mountains, with fewer cities, smaller towns, and a lot fewer people living there.

Because of its long and varied history, Massachusetts has a lot of places listed on the National Register of Historic Places, including three national historical parks: Lowell, Boston, and Minute Man.

Massachusetts is also home to many ponds and small lakes, such as the famous Walden Pond and Lake Chargogg.

Massachusetts has a lot of islands off of its coast, including such large ones as Nantucket and Martha's Vineyard. Rivers such

Maple Magic

Starting at number 1,
connect the dots in order
to find a maple surprise.

EXTRA FUN: Take the total number of dots and divide by 2.
This is how many gallons of sap from a maple tree it takes to
make one gallon of pure New England maple syrup!

WORDS TO KNOW

Lake Chargoggmaunchaugag-oggchaubungungamaugg

This is the longest name of any body of water in the United States. It is a Native American name that means "You fish on your side and I'll fish on my side, and nobody fishes in the middle," and was probably named in honor of an agreement between two tribes on how best to peacefully share access to it.

as the Merrimack are short and speedy, and helped provide the waterpower that the early textile mills of the 1800s needed in order to run faster than any had before. These textile mills were part of the Industrial Revolution in America.

Massachusetts' economy relies heavily on industry. In other words, a lot of the people who live in Massachusetts make things for a living. Electronic items like computer parts, electrical wires and cords, plus tools, a lot of plastics, and many other manufactured things are all made in Massachusetts. Massachusetts has so much manufacturing within its borders partly because when industries began to manufacture goods in the modern way, Massachusetts was one of the first places where companies set up modern plants with assembly lines.

History

The Commonwealth of Massachusetts is one of the original thirteen states, and the second oldest of the English colonies (after Virginia). Its capital city of Boston was founded in 1630 by Puritans seeking religious freedom.

The Puritans were a group of people who came from England to America because of their religious differences with England's official church, the Anglican Church. Originally, this group of people hoped to "purify" the Anglican Church of some of its religious practices that they didn't like. This is how they got the nickname "Puritans." Today the spiritual descendants of the Puritans are members of the Episcopalian Church of America.

Massachusetts has a rich history, and has many interesting things to see if you go visit, such as the battlefields of Lexington and Concord, where the American Revolution started. Also, the U.S. Navy's oldest active commissioned warship, a sailing vessel called the USS Constitution, is permanently docked in Boston Harbor. She is over two hundred years old!

RHODE ISLAND: The Ocean State
Geography and Industry

With a total area of 1,214 square miles, Rhode Island is the smallest of the fifty states. Also, after New Jersey, it is the most densely populated state, in spite of the fact that much of the western part of the state is heavily forested. Rhode Island is made up mostly of the land surrounding the large waterway known as Narragansett Bay (and the islands in it).

There is a lot to see and do in Rhode Island. The seaside community of Newport is world-famous for its history of yachting, and there are some amazing homes to visit there, including the ones built by the wealthy Vanderbilt family. In fact, with its miles and miles of coastline, Rhode Island has more oceanfront than some states twice its size!

Like Massachusetts to the north, Rhode Island's economy relies heavily on manufacturing. Industries represented within the state include textiles, jewelry making, electrical wire and cable manufacturing, and some agriculture. Fishing was once the most important industry in the state, but it no longer is, because it is not as profitable as it once was. Narragansett Bay is still home to a plentiful amount of shellfish.

Even though commercial fishing isn't as important as it once was, shipping is still a major industry in Rhode Island. After all, Narragansett Bay is a fine natural harbor.

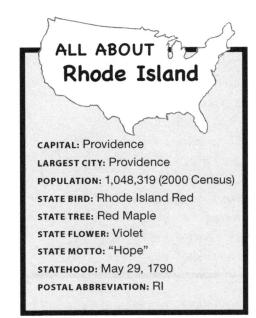

ALL ABOUT Rhode Island

CAPITAL: Providence
LARGEST CITY: Providence
POPULATION: 1,048,319 (2000 Census)
STATE BIRD: Rhode Island Red
STATE TREE: Red Maple
STATE FLOWER: Violet
STATE MOTTO: "Hope"
STATEHOOD: May 29, 1790
POSTAL ABBREVIATION: RI

History

Rhode Island was first settled in 1636 by followers of a Puritan leader named Roger Williams. Williams had been banished from nearby Massachusetts because he preached that people ought to tolerate each other's religious differences. Later Anne Hutchinson likewise angered leaders of the Plymouth colony and was also banished. She also moved to Rhode Island in search of religious freedom and founded the present site of Portsmouth. As a result, Rhode Island is seen by many as the cradle of America's tradition of religious freedom.

WORDS TO KNOW

Textiles

Textile refers to both a number of types of finished cloth and also the fibers or yarns from which they are made. Items like cotton shirts, tablecloths, and carpets are referred to as textiles.

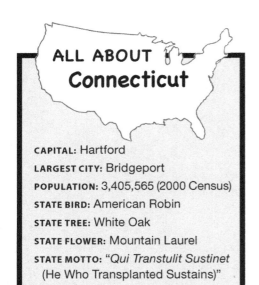

ALL ABOUT Connecticut

CAPITAL: Hartford

LARGEST CITY: Bridgeport

POPULATION: 3,405,565 (2000 Census)

STATE BIRD: American Robin

STATE TREE: White Oak

STATE FLOWER: Mountain Laurel

STATE MOTTO: *"Qui Transtulit Sustinet (He Who Transplanted Sustains)"*

STATEHOOD: January 9, 1788

POSTAL ABBREVIATION: CT

At the start of the Revolutionary War, Rhode Islanders were the first colonists to reject their allegiance to Britain and were also the first colonists to take action against the British by attacking British vessels. Although no large battles were fought in Rhode Island, regiments from the state participated in every major campaign in the war.

After the American Revolution, the shipping industry declined in Rhode Island. But Samuel Slater soon founded the first successful U.S. textile mill on the banks of the Blackstone River in what is today Pawtucket, Rhode Island. The abundance of waterpower at the site led to the rapid development of manufacturing, which is considered to be the start of the Industrial Revolution in the United States.

CONNECTICUT: The Constitution State
Geography and Industry

The Connecticut River (for which the state is named) runs through the middle of this state, cutting it in two. The Connecticut River Valley separates Connecticut's Eastern Highland from its Western Highland.

Connecticut was one of the original thirteen colonies that formed the early United States. Initially settled by Dutch traders beginning in the mid-1630s, then by Pilgrims from Plymouth Colony, and eventually by Puritans from Massachusetts Bay, Connecticut incorporated as an English royal colony by writing up the Fundamental Orders (the colony's main set of governing laws) in 1639. These laws were eventually replaced by a formal, written constitution in 1662.

Like its neighbors Massachusetts and Rhode Island, Connecticut is an important manufacturing center. Sewing machines, textiles, firearms, and heavy machinery, including engine parts, are all made in Connecticut. (Guns have been made continuously in Connecticut since the American Revolution!) Although farming is no longer a major industry in Connecticut, apples, dairy products, eggs, tobacco, and mushrooms are all still grown there and shipped around the country.

History

Two of early America's most savage Indian wars took place in Connecticut. First came the Pequot War, named for the largest and most powerful tribe of Native Americans in the area. It broke out in 1637 between the Pequot tribe and the Connecticut and Massachusetts Bay colonies (along with some Native Americans who fought with the colonists). The war ended with the virtual extinction of the Pequots.

The second of Connecticut's bloody Indian wars was King Philip's War, which began in 1674 in Connecticut and quickly spread throughout the New England colonies. Fought between the formerly friendly Wampanoag tribe and the English settlers, it also ended badly for the Native Americans. Thousands of them died or lost their homes.

NEW HAMPSHIRE: The Granite State

Geography

New Hampshire is bordered to the north by the Canadian province of Quebec. Maine borders New Hampshire to the east, Massachusetts to the south, and Vermont to the west. The Connecticut River forms the border between New Hampshire and Vermont.

New Hampshire is very mountainous and is home to the tallest mountain east of the Rocky Mountains: Mount Washington, which is 6,288 feet above sea level. Some of the best skiing in the eastern United States can be found in New Hampshire!

History

The last of the original thirteen colonies to be established (in 1741, when it broke away from Massachusetts Bay), New Hampshire was the first of the future United States to declare its independence from Great Britain. Famous for its state motto ("Live

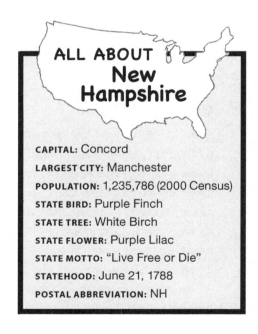

ALL ABOUT New Hampshire

CAPITAL: Concord
LARGEST CITY: Manchester
POPULATION: 1,235,786 (2000 Census)
STATE BIRD: Purple Finch
STATE TREE: White Birch
STATE FLOWER: Purple Lilac
STATE MOTTO: "Live Free or Die"
STATEHOOD: June 21, 1788
POSTAL ABBREVIATION: NH

Free or Die") and for the White Mountains that run through it, New Hampshire is a state that prides itself on being very different even from its neighbors in New England.

One of the most important things to happen in New Hampshire after the American Revolution was the negotiation and signing of the Treaty of Portsmouth in 1905. Negotiated by President Theodore Roosevelt, the Treaty of Portsmouth ended the Russo-Japanese War (a war between Russia and Japan). This treaty not only ensured Japan's new status as a world power, but also showed that the United States was a powerful country that would use its own emerging world power status to help keep the peace from continent to continent.

Economy

New Hampshire began using the water in its rivers to power textile mills during the 1800s, as part of the beginning of the Industrial Revolution. These days, although much of the manufacturing in the state has shifted to high-technology supplies, there are still many manufacturers of leather goods, particularly of shoes and boots.

In recent years, tourism has become one of the most important industries in New Hampshire. During the winter months, people come from all over the country to ski in New Hampshire's rugged mountains. During the summers, the state's lakes, such as the huge Winnipeesaukee, are home to summer boaters. Fishing is no longer as important as it once was in the state, but still plays a role in the state's economy.

Two other industries that were once of major importance in New Hampshire are the lumber industry and the granite quarrying industry. The lumber harvested in New Hampshire is used in making paper. Lumber is about the only harvesting going on in New Hampshire. The mountains and the thin, flinty soil make it tough to grow food there. As for the granite quarrying industry, there is not as much demand for granite as a building material as there used to be. Steel makes up the foundations of most buildings nowadays.

Fun Facts

THE OLD MAN OF THE MOUNTAIN

The Old Man of the Mountain was a New Hampshire rock formation that looked very much like the profile of an old man. New Hampshire residents came to identify with this rock outcropping, and adopted it as their state symbol in 1945. The rocks that formed the natural sculpture had weathered over the years, though, and the entire structure collapsed in 2003.

Yee Ha!

They were hand crafted in Concord, NH, but were famous for carrying mail and passengers throughout the western United States! Can you help this Concord Coach deliver the mail from START to END of the route?

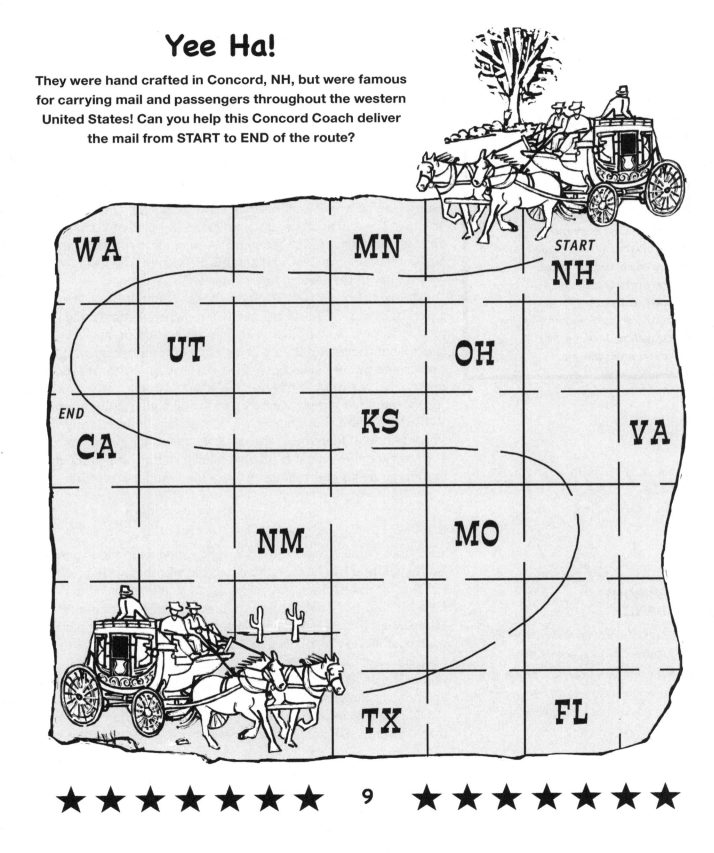

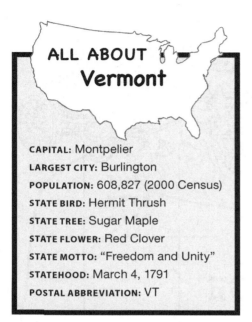

ALL ABOUT Vermont

CAPITAL: Montpelier

LARGEST CITY: Burlington

POPULATION: 608,827 (2000 Census)

STATE BIRD: Hermit Thrush

STATE TREE: Sugar Maple

STATE FLOWER: Red Clover

STATE MOTTO: "Freedom and Unity"

STATEHOOD: March 4, 1791

POSTAL ABBREVIATION: VT

Fun Facts

VERMONT GRANITE

Vermont's granite and marble quarries produce some of the most distinctive building stone in the world. Vermont marble in particular is thought to rival Italian marble in its beauty.

VERMONT: The Green Mountain State

Geography and Industry

Bordered on two sides by large bodies of fresh water, Vermont shares its western border with New York (where Lake Champlain forms part of the boundary), and its eastern border with New Hampshire (where the Connecticut River marks the entire boundary line). The Canadian province of Quebec is north of Vermont, and Massachusetts lies to the south. Vermont is a very mountainous state. Vermont's Green Mountains are some of the most rugged country in the eastern United States.

Unlike the other New England states, Vermont has a strong agricultural base. This is especially true when it comes to dairy products. Vermont's milk and cheese are world famous—as is Vermont ice cream! (Ben & Jerry's is a Vermont company.) Apples and maple syrup are also important agricultural products that come from Vermont.

Vermont has a reputation for producing high-quality marble. While New Hampshire marble was valuable in building early skyscrapers and millionaires' mansions, Vermont marble comes in so many varieties that it is highly prized as a finishing product (as in marble tile for bathrooms) and as a medium for sculpture.

History

Vermont's contribution to the Patriot cause during the American Revolution can be traced back to the very beginning of the war for independence. On May 10, 1775, Vermont militiamen (the famous Green Mountain Boys) under the command of Ethan Allen and Benedict Arnold seized Fort Ticonderoga (which controlled access to all of Lake Champlain) in the name of the new Continental Congress. They did so without firing a shot, taking the British garrison there completely by surprise during an early morning raid.

During the decades leading up to the American Revolution, three different English colonies (New York, New Hampshire, and

Massachusetts Bay) claimed the area now known as the state of Vermont as part of their own territories. As a result of their inability to settle their differences over Vermont, these three colonies blocked Vermont's attempts to join the United States as a new state during the late 1770s.

In response to this dilemma, Vermont declared itself an independent state. The state's government coined its own money, appointed ambassadors, set up a postal system, and did all the everyday functions of an independent government until finally allowed to join the Union as the first state that had not previously been an English colony (and the fourteenth state overall).

MAINE: The Pine Tree State
Geography and Industry

Maine's soil is rocky, and not very good for raising crops. The state originally had large forests filled with huge pine trees, but heavy logging has cleared much of the land. There is still plenty of wilderness to be explored in Maine, though, especially in the northern parts of the state. People come from all over the world to camp and hike in Maine's forests of white pine, and to boat and fish not only in its 5,500 lakes and streams but also on its irregular, rock-strewn, 3,500 miles of coastline.

Maine's economy relies heavily on timber sales, but not in the same way that it did when tall Maine trees were cut down to make ships' masts. Nowadays, Maine's trees are used mostly as pulp to make paper.

At one time, fishing was Maine's largest and richest industry. But the fishing industry has suffered recently, because the supply of fish is getting smaller. Many environmentalists think this is a result of what is called over-fishing. Over-fishing is what happens when fishermen don't leave enough of a type of fish for that species of fish to produce enough new fish to replace those that were caught that year. One exception to the over-fishing problem is the famous Maine lobster which is sold worldwide.

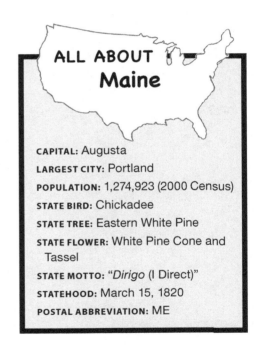

ALL ABOUT Maine

CAPITAL: Augusta

LARGEST CITY: Portland

POPULATION: 1,274,923 (2000 Census)

STATE BIRD: Chickadee

STATE TREE: Eastern White Pine

STATE FLOWER: White Pine Cone and Tassel

STATE MOTTO: *"Dirigo* (I Direct)"

STATEHOOD: March 15, 1820

POSTAL ABBREVIATION: ME

Fun Facts

MAINE'S TIMBER INDUSTRY

Timber has always been a major export for Maine. During the Age of Sail (when people traveled mostly by sailing ships), Maine's tall white pine trees were used to make ships' masts, which hold up the sails. In fact, the very first sawmill in the United States was built in Maine, on the Piscataqua River in 1623.

History

Up until 1820, Maine was a part of Massachusetts. In that year Maine entered the Union as a free state (meaning that slavery was illegal in the state), as part of a deal made in Congress between representatives of southern and northern states, called the Missouri Compromise. The Missouri Compromise was an agreement that allowed Missouri to enter the Union as a slave state). Since Maine would enter the Union at the same time, it would help keep the number of slave and free states in the Union equal. During the 1830s, Maine was the site of a border dispute between the United States and Canada. This conflict, called the Aroostook War, resulted in no deaths, and only a few bruises among the men who "fought" it. The long-term result of this so-called war was the Webster-Ashburton Treaty of 1842, which settled the boundary line between the United States and Canada not only in Maine, but along most of the rest of the border as well, making it the longest undefended international border in world history.

CHAPTER 2
THE MID-ATLANTIC STATES

Fun Facts

NIAGARA FALLS

The falls of the Niagara River are a world-famous attraction that draws millions of people to see them every year. Every hour 5,000,000,000 gallons of water flow over the edge of the Niagara Falls.

WORDS TO KNOW

Floodplain

A floodplain is a flat piece of land next to a river, stream, or ocean that experiences occasional flooding.

The states in the Mid-Atlantic region run from New York in the north along the Atlantic shore of the east coast, to the Potomac River in the south. All five of the states in this region were among the original thirteen colonies that fought for independence from Great Britain and later ratified the U.S. Constitution.

The Mid-Atlantic States were also the birthplace of the westward settlement movement and the Transportation Revolution (1816–1850). These two sweeping events led to the beginnings of the railway, steel, coal, oil, and canal-building industries. As a result, some of the largest and most heavily populated cities in the United States are in the Mid-Atlantic States. Cities such as New York City, Philadelphia, Buffalo, Pittsburgh, and Baltimore all boomed in part because of their location during the Transportation Revolution.

NEW YORK: The Empire State
Geography and Industry

In the southeast, New York's Long Island is surrounded by three bodies of water: Long Island Sound, the Atlantic Ocean, and New York Harbor. Along its southern border, New York is bordered by New Jersey and Pennsylvania.

New York has a little bit of every terrain, except for desert, within its borders. In the southeast, there is the broad floodplain of the Atlantic. Running north from there is the Great Appalachian Valley, which includes the Hudson River and Lake Champlain. The Hudson cuts through the Allegheny Plateau, which rises into the Catskill Mountains.

The northern part of the state is mountainous, with the Adirondack chain running through it. Western New York is very hilly, with a number of lakes, including the Finger Lakes and Lake Oneida.

History

Before European settlement, New York was the home of many different tribes of Native Americans. The most powerful tribes were the Iroquois confederacy in western New York.

The Iroquois were not one tribe—they were actually five tribes! They called themselves the *Ho-de-no-sau-nee*, which means "People of the Longhouse." In the minds of the Iroquois, they all lived together, much the same way that a family will live in different parts of a house today. The Seneca lived furthest west, and were called the Keepers of the Western Door. The Mohawks lived furthest east, and were called the Keepers of the Eastern Door. The tribes in the middle were the Cayuga, Oneida, and Onondaga. Many of the descendants of the Iroquois still live in western New York as well as in southern Canada today.

The French and Dutch were the first Europeans to visit New York. They have left their words as place names all over the state—for example, bodies of water like Lake Champlain (pronounced "sham-PLAIN") and the Schuylkill River (pronounced "SKOOL-kil").

The Dutch (people from the Netherlands) founded the first permanent settlement in what is now New York when they bought an island at the mouth of the Hudson River in 1626. They paid local Native Americans with trade goods (blankets and colored beads) that would cost us about $25.00 in today's money for what is now Manhattan Island! Imagine buying the area where New York City now stands, and having money left over from your allowance. You'd be the next Donald Trump!

The Dutch called this colony New Netherlands, and called the city they built on Manhattan Island New Amsterdam. The English later fought a war with the Dutch and took New Netherlands away from them. They changed the name of the colony (and its largest city) to New York.

After America became a nation, New York City quickly became more and more important. It was even the national capital city for a brief time! Did you know that when New York became a state, the northern parts of Manhattan Island still had farms on them? It's true! But by the late nineteenth century, with the growth of manufacturing in New York City, the farms were long gone.

One of the major reasons for New York's emergence as the foremost city of the new nation was its harbor, lauded by

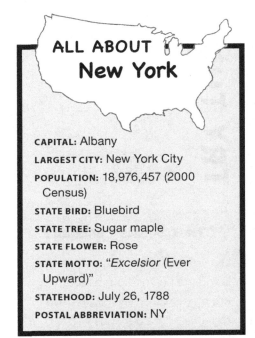

ALL ABOUT New York

CAPITAL: Albany

LARGEST CITY: New York City

POPULATION: 18,976,457 (2000 Census)

STATE BIRD: Bluebird

STATE TREE: Sugar maple

STATE FLOWER: Rose

STATE MOTTO: "*Excelsior* (Ever Upward)"

STATEHOOD: July 26, 1788

POSTAL ABBREVIATION: NY

The Iroquois Language

Did you know that the Iroquois language has no sounds that are made with your lips pressed together? It's true! Their names for themselves, as well as the rest of their language, do not include sounds like "m," "b," or "p." That is why they have names like Ho-de-no-sau-nee, and Hiawatha, and Thayendaneegeeah. Try saying these names without touching your lips together. Can you do it?

many as the finest natural harbor in the western hemisphere. This meant a boom in the trade that passed through New York City on its way between the American West and places overseas such as Europe and Asia. On top of the city's harbor, there also was the fact that New York state had built the famous Erie Canal, which made it very easy to get trade goods back and forth across the state between the harbor cities of New York, which was on the Atlantic coast, and Buffalo, which serves as an important port city at the eastern end of the Great Lakes.

PENNSYLVANIA: The Keystone State
Geography and Industry

The Appalachian Mountains pass right through the heart of Pennsylvania. With the Delaware River Valley helping form the eastern part of the state, Pennsylvania has everything from rugged mountains to smooth river bottoms.

But Pennsylvania isn't just a land of mountains and plains. It is also a land of large rivers. Along with the large and powerful Delaware (and the Susquehanna, which flows through the state and down into the Chesapeake Bay), Pennsylvania also has the mighty Ohio River, which begins in the western part of the state. In fact, the Ohio begins right in the middle of what is now the city of Pittsburgh! The city was originally the site of a fort built where the Monongahela and Allegheny rivers merge to form the Ohio River. This is where Pittsburgh's once famous Three Rivers football stadium got its name!

History

There were many powerful tribes of Native Americans living in what is now Pennsylvania before European settlement. These included the Delaware, the Suquehannock, and the Shawnee.

Many people don't know that there were more Europeans exploring and colonizing the New World than just the French,

English, and Spanish. In Pennsylvania and neighboring New Jersey, two other countries struggled to control new colonies: the Swedish and the Dutch!

The Swedes were forced out by the Dutch, who were then forced out by the English. The Duke of York (the brother of the English king) gave Pennsylvania to an English Quaker named William Penn. Why did he just give all this land away? It's because he owed Penn money! So he gave away a colony that English soldiers had taken away from the Dutch a few years before. Penn asked for the land as payment of the debt, because he wanted to start a colony there for other Quakers.

Pennsylvania was very important during the American Revolution. Everyone knows that the Declaration of Independence was signed on July 4, 1776. But do you know *where* it was signed? The Declaration of Independence was signed at Independence Hall in Philadelphia, Pennsylvania, and that place is now a national historical landmark. American and British forces fought a number of battles in Pennsylvania during the Revolution, at places including Brandywine and Germantown. Congress was forced to flee Philadelphia when the British army invaded Pennsylvania and captured the city. In order to keep an eye on the British, General Washington's Continental Army spent a terrible winter not far away, at Valley Forge.

Since the American Revolution, Pennsylvania has been an integral part of the Industrial Revolution. After all, the state is the site of the first oil well in the United States. It also has some of the largest coal deposits in the world. When the Industrial Revolution began, Pennsylvania was an ideal place for steel mills to spring up because the state had plenty of coal to power the mills. Men like Andrew Carnegie made millions from building up the steel industry, mostly in Pennsylvania!

You might know Andrew Carnegie's name because when he died he left most of his money to a fund that set up free public libraries all over the country. Many cities and towns that couldn't have afforded a library otherwise had one as a result of his generosity. Is there a Carnegie Library where you live?

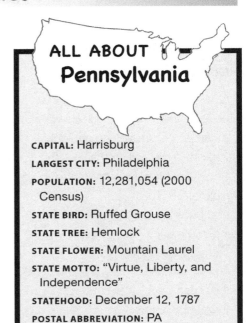

ALL ABOUT Pennsylvania

CAPITAL: Harrisburg

LARGEST CITY: Philadelphia

POPULATION: 12,281,054 (2000 Census)

STATE BIRD: Ruffed Grouse

STATE TREE: Hemlock

STATE FLOWER: Mountain Laurel

STATE MOTTO: "Virtue, Liberty, and Independence"

STATEHOOD: December 12, 1787

POSTAL ABBREVIATION: PA

Fun Facts

PHILADELPHIA, OUR CAPITAL!

Did you know that Philadelphia was the first capital of the United States? It's true! For a number of years both during and after the American Revolution, Philadelphia was our national capital. The capital moved to New York during President Washington's administration.

WORDS TO KNOW

Quaker

Quakers are a religious group that believes that everything in life was meant to be simple and straightforward. They call themselves the Society of Friends, and got the nickname "Quakers" because during some early sermons preached among some of their members, the people shook violently while "possessed by the Holy Spirit"!

ALL ABOUT New Jersey

CAPITAL: Trenton

LARGEST CITY: Newark

POPULATION: 8,414,350 (2000 Census)

STATE BIRD: Eastern Goldfinch

STATE TREE: Red Oak

STATE FLOWER: Purple Violet

STATE MOTTO: "Liberty and Prosperity"

STATEHOOD: December 18, 1787

POSTAL ABBREVIATION: NJ

NEW JERSEY: The Garden State
Geography and Industry

New Jersey shares its northern border with New York. Aside from that, all of its other borders are formed by water: the Delaware River to the west, the Atlantic Ocean to the east, and Delaware Bay to the south. Northern New Jersey is very hilly, and southern New Jersey is very flat. The big rivers running through New Jersey are the Passaic and the Raritan.

New Jersey is one of the smallest of the United States (only Rhode Island, Massachusetts, Connecticut, and Delaware are smaller), but it is also one of the most populous. This means that New Jersey has a lot of people living in its borders. New Jersey ranks in the top ten of all the states in population numbers. That is a lot of people living in a very narrow space! New Jersey is a very crowded state in part because it is right between the huge eastern cities of Philadelphia and New York City. In fact, the metropolitan areas of both of these cities have expanded into New Jersey over the last few decades. As a result of this, many of the residents of New Jersey commute to jobs in other states!

History

Remember how eastern Pennsylvania was originally settled by the Swedes (people from Sweden)? Well, the same thing happened in New Jersey, which is just on the other side of the Delaware River from Pennsylvania. And just like in Pennsylvania, the Swedes were forced out by the Dutch, who after a few years lost a war with the English, who then claimed New Jersey and Pennsylvania for themselves. The Dutch left their mark in this area through the names of villages such as Hoboken (which is a large city today).

Two of the most important battles of the American Revolution were fought in New Jersey. Have you learned in school about General Washington's famous crossing of the Delaware? Maybe you've

seen the famous painting, which shows him and his soldiers crossing the river in big boats. If you have, did you wonder where he was going when he and his army crossed the river?

Well, the answer is that he was going to New Jersey! Washington's army crossed the Delaware the night before Christmas, and attacked Hessian soldiers the next morning in their camp at Trenton. He and his troops took the Hessians completely by surprise, killed many soldiers, and captured many others. A few days later, Washington struck again, this time at Princeton, New Jersey (now home of the famous university that bears its name), and again won an overwhelming victory! These two battles were very important because up to that point, General Washington had not won many battles against either the British or the Hessians, and his winning at Trenton and Princeton gave the patriots everywhere hope that they would win independence from England.

New Jerseyite of Note

One of the ways in which New Jersey has had a major impact on the world since the end of the American Revolution was by helping launch the motion picture industry. Did you know that before there was a Hollywood, there was a Menlo Park? Menlo Park, New Jersey, that is. It's true, the first American movies were filmed in New Jersey!

And guess who filmed many of those movies? Thomas Edison. Have you heard of him? Yes, he invented the light bulb (well, he actually improved the design of another scientist, allowing a light bulb to burn for longer than a few minutes before it burned out), but he did much more, and he did it all in his laboratory in Menlo Park, New Jersey. In fact, one of his many nicknames was "the wizard of Menlo Park."

Aside from improving the light bulb, Edison also invented the phonograph (an old-fashioned record player). Ask your parents or grandparents what a

WORDS TO KNOW

Hessians

Hessians were soldiers from Hesse-Cassel (pronounced "hess-CASS-ul"), a region of what is now Germany. Their king "rented" their services out to the English king, King George III. In exchange for the money that George III paid the Hessian ruler, these soldiers came to America to fight against the rebelling colonists.

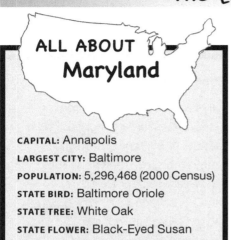

ALL ABOUT Maryland

CAPITAL: Annapolis

LARGEST CITY: Baltimore

POPULATION: 5,296,468 (2000 Census)

STATE BIRD: Baltimore Oriole

STATE TREE: White Oak

STATE FLOWER: Black-Eyed Susan

STATE MOTTO: "*Fatti Maschii, Parole Femine* (Manly Deeds, Womanly Words)"

STATEHOOD: April 28, 1788

POSTAL ABBREVIATION: MD

TRY THIS!

Maryland Seafood

Have you ever had a crab cake? The next time you go to the grocery store with your parents, find the crab cakes and see if you can find on their packaging where they were made. If they came from Maryland they're probably the best you'll ever eat!

phonograph is. They might even have one they can show to you. Phonograph records work a lot differently than CDs and MP3s work today! Other inventions that Edison improved include the typewriter, which did some of the things that computers do today (again, ask your parents or grandparents) and the motion picture camera. Some of the oldest home movies ever taken were shot in the 1890s in New Jersey, in and around Edison's laboratory in Menlo Park. In fact, Edison even started the first movie studio. When movies began to be shown around the country a few years later, many people called them "Edison shows."

MARYLAND: The Old Line State
Geography

Maryland is cut in two, right down the middle, by a huge body of water called the Chesapeake Bay. The part of the state that is separated from the rest of it by the big bay is called the Eastern Shore. The state shares its eastern border with Delaware and the Atlantic Ocean. To the north lies Pennsylvania, to the south is Virginia, and to the west is West Virginia. Between Maryland and Virginia is the District of Columbia, where the U.S. capital of Washington, D.C. is located. The state has many different types of landscapes. In the east and the southeast it is very flat, with lots of good farming land. The Piedmont (a chain of mountains) runs through the western part of the state, making it far more rugged than the eastern and the central parts.

History

Maryland was originally a colony run by Lord Baltimore, an English lord who named the colony for his wife and the largest city in it for his family. Lord Baltimore wanted a place that would welcome Catholics. At the time, Catholics were not treated very well back home in England. Although people of many faiths eventually settled in Maryland, it shared Rhode Island's beginning as a safe haven where people could worship as they chose.

Did you know that Maryland almost joined the Confederate States of America? It's true! Maryland was a southern state, where tobacco and cotton were grown and where slavery was legal. Many Marylanders thought that their place was fighting with their neighbors to the south against the northern states. In fact, many Marylanders fought on the southern side during the Civil War, even though their state never actually officially left the union!

One of these men who believed in the southern cause was a famous actor named John Wilkes Booth, who later shocked the country and the world by shooting and killing our sixteenth president, Abraham Lincoln. Booth often referred to the south as his home, and to slavery as a God-given right. No wonder he hated President Lincoln!

ALL ABOUT Delaware

CAPITAL: Dover
LARGEST CITY: Wilmington
POPULATION: 783,600 (2000 Census)
STATE BIRD: Blue Hen Chicken
STATE TREE: American Holly
STATE FLOWER: Peach Blossom
STATE MOTTO: "Liberty and Independence"
STATEHOOD: December 7, 1787
POSTAL ABBREVIATION: DE

DELAWARE: The Diamond State
Geography and Industry

Delaware occupies the northern and eastern portion of what many Marylanders call the Eastern Shore, and what still others call the Delmarva peninsula (short for Delaware-Maryland-Virginia). It is one of the smallest peninsulas of the United States.

Have you ever heard of the DuPont Corporation? It's a company that makes lots of things, especially all kinds of plastic, plastic tools, and paint. The DuPont Corporation is a big business with its headquarters in Delaware, where a man named Pierre DuPont started it. His great-grandson, Pierre "Pete" DuPont IV, eventually became a congressman from Delaware, as well as a governor of the state.

History

Before European settlement, most of what is now Delaware was occupied by members of the Delaware tribe of Native Americans. In 1610 an English explorer named one of Delaware's capes "La Warre," in honor of Virginia Colony's governor, Baron de La Warr. This is where the name "Delaware" comes from.

As you learned in reading about New Jersey and Pennsylvania, the first Europeans to settle in the Delaware River Valley

Fun Facts

THE FIRST STATE!

Did you know that Delaware was the first of the original thirteen colonies (later the first thirteen states) that won their independence from England to ratify the U.S. Constitution? It's true! The people of Delaware are to this day very proud to call theirs the "first state," because of this!

State to State

Choose the state names that complete the silly riddles.

HINT: **The pictures are a clue.**

New York   Utah
Maryland   Idaho
New Jersey   Delaware
Pennsylvania

What did

_____?

She wore her

_____!

What did

_____?

She hoed her

_____!

were the Swedes and the Dutch. In fact, Peter Minuit, who had once been the governor of New Netherlands (modern New York), was hired by Sweden to establish a colony in the New World. He established Fort Christina (named for Sweden's queen) on the present site of the city of Wilmington, Delaware, in 1631.

This brought the Swedish traders who came to settle around the colony into conflict with the Dutch, who had already claimed the entire Delaware Valley as their own. They fought a war with the Swedes that ended in 1654. The Swedes lost. Ten years later, the Dutch lost all of their possessions in North America to the English. England's king gave all of these lands, which included all of what is now Delaware, to the Duke of York.

For most of the rest of the colonial era, Delaware was a semi-independent part of the Pennsylvania colony. A few years later, Delaware became an English crown colony.

During the American Revolution, Delaware contributed many brave soldiers to the Continental Army. They became known as the Blue Hen's Chickens, because they fought with the ferocity of gamecocks.

WORDS TO KNOW

Gamecock

A gamecock is a rooster (male) chicken, usually bred to be an aggressive fighter. Before such things were outlawed, gamecocks were used in rooster fights (called cock fights), which people would bet money on.

CHAPTER 3

THE UPPER SOUTH

Have you ever had Kentucky Fried Chicken? Well, can you guess where it originally came from? The Upper South is where much of what is called "southern cooking" comes from. Recipes for meals like mac 'n' cheese, chicken and dumplings, and fried chicken were created in this region.

Some of the states in the Upper South have been called the Border States, because they run along the Mason-Dixon Line, which runs along Pennsylvania's border with Maryland, then along the Ohio River, all the way to the Mississippi. This line was originally established to end an argument over state boundaries between Maryland and Pennsylvania. But it is also well known for dividing the free states from the slave states until the Civil War.

All of these Border States participated in the Civil War, and almost all of them had their citizens fighting on both sides in that terrible struggle. The main reasons the Civil War was fought between the North and the South were questions like whether individual states had the right to make laws that were not allowed by the national government, and whether the practice of slavery ought to be protected (as many Southerners thought) or whether it ought to be abolished (as many Northerners thought).

ALL ABOUT Virginia

CAPITAL: Richmond

LARGEST CITY: Virginia Beach

POPULATION: 7,078,515 (2000 Census)

STATE BIRD: Cardinal

STATE TREE: Dogwood

STATE FLOWER: Dogwood

STATE MOTTO: "*Sic Semper Tyrannis* (Thus Always to Tyrants)"

STATEHOOD: June 25, 1788

POSTAL ABBREVIATION: VA

VIRGINIA: The Old Dominion State

Geography and Industry

Virginia is a very large state now, but in the past it was even larger. Virginia once claimed all of the land that now makes up two different states, West Virginia and Kentucky, in addition to its present territory! In 1792, Congress created the state of Kentucky in the west, and in 1863, northwestern Virginia seceded from the rest of the state to form West Virginia.

Eastern Virginia is made up of the southern tip of the Delmarva Peninsula (named for the three states that share it: Delaware, Maryland, and Virginia) and a few islands in between the Atlantic Ocean and the Chesapeake Bay. This region is also called the Eastern Shore.

The central part of Virginia includes two types of country. The tidewater section, which is right on the shore of Chesapeake Bay, is flat, humid, and very swampy in many places. Four big rivers run through the tidewater section: the James (where Jamestown is), the York, the Rappahannock, and the Potomac.

The other type of country in the central part of Virginia is called the Piedmont. The Piedmont is hillier than the flat tidewater section, and has a lot of fertile soil. Everything from wheat to gourds like squash and pumpkins to tobacco is grown in the Piedmont. Cattle are also raised there. The Piedmont rises higher and higher as it goes west, until it becomes the mountains of the Blue Ridge. The western part of Virginia is very rugged.

History

Many Native American tribes lived in Virginia before Europeans visited the region. The Powhatan confederacy was the largest group of native tribes in the area when English settlers landed at what is now Jamestown in 1607. They took their name from their leader, Powhatan. You have heard of Pocahontas, haven't you? Well, Pocahontas was Chief Powhatan's daughter.

When English ships first landed in Virginia in 1607, most of the men who came as part of the expedition were interested in one thing: gold! They had heard that in the New World, gold and silver were just lying around on the ground, waiting to be picked up.

At first, the members of the tiny new colony were only interested in finding the kind of treasure the Spanish had found in Mexico and Peru. They were so busy looking for it that they didn't bother to farm, trade for food, or raise livestock. As a result, they nearly starved to death.

But later generations learned a lesson from what the original settlers called the "starving time." They came to realize that in Virginia, it was easier to grow tobacco than to find gold. They could also grow wheat that would sell for good prices. By the time the American Revolution started, Virginia was a very prosperous colony.

TRY THIS!

Can you tell the difference between a pumpkin and a squash?

The plants themselves, not their fruit! Both plants are members of the gourd family. The next time you go to pick out a pumpkin for Halloween, ask the farmer if you can see his pumpkin patch. What types of plants are pumpkin plants? Are they bushes or vines? And what about squash? If you can't go to the country to try this, you can always look on the Internet.

WORDS TO KNOW

Powhatan

The powerful chief of the Powhatan confederacy of Native American tribes, this man was also the father of the famous Pocahontas. Actually, "Powhatan" was a title, like "king." Powhatan's real name was Wahunsonacock.

Virginia

When the English first landed in Virginia, they named their new colony in honor of their ruler, Queen Elizabeth I. People called Elizabeth I the Virgin Queen, which is how the settlers came up with the name Virginia.

Important Virginians

Four of the first five presidents of the United States were Virginians! These great men were George Washington, Thomas Jefferson, James Madison, and James Monroe. All of these future presidents contributed to the American cause of getting independence from the British during the Revolution. Washington was commander-in-chief of the Continental Army. He is largely credited with keeping his army going during the early years of the Revolution, when they were losing battle after battle.

Jefferson served in the Continental Congress, and wrote most of the Declaration of Independence. Jefferson was also America's first secretary of state (an official who takes care of this country's relationships with other countries), and also served as vice president before he became president in 1801.

Madison also served in the Congress, and was largely responsible for the U.S. Constitution (the system of government we still have in this country today). Madison is the man who came up with the idea of making the president, the Congress, and the Supreme Court equal branches of government, in order to make sure that one person didn't have too much power and become a tyrant.

Monroe served as an officer under Washington's command in the Continental Army, and later as a diplomat in Europe, negotiating treaties and trade agreements with other countries for the new American government.

Virginia and the Civil War

Virginia's location played a big part in the state's being the site of many of the major battles of the American Civil War. This was partly because Virginia was the northernmost state to secede from the Union and join the Confederacy, and partly because it was across the Potomac River from the Union capital of Washington, D.C. Also, after Virginia seceded, the Confederate capital moved to its largest city, Richmond. This placed the capital cities of both sides in the war within 100 miles of each other.

Many men from Virginia served on both sides during the Civil War. One of them was General Robert E. Lee, who resigned from the Union Army and went on to command the Confederate Army. Before he resigned his commission, he turned down President Lincoln's offer of command of the Union Army. When asked why he did not take the president's offer, Lee said, "I cannot go against my country." By that he meant Virginia.

WEST VIRGINIA: The Mountain State
Geography and Industry

West Virginia is one of the most heavily forested and most rugged of all the states east of the Mississippi River. Almost all of West Virginia is located on the Allegheny Plateau, which is a high stretch of land with a pretty flat top (as opposed to mountain ranges, which do not have flat tops). Fast-flowing rivers like the Big Sandy, the Kanawha, and the Monongahela cut through parts of West Virginia. The northern part is not on the plateau at all. It is part of the Ohio River Valley (the Ohio River runs along West Virginia's northwestern border).

Because of its high elevation, West Virginia gets a lot of snow every winter, and that in turn draws crowds of skiers every year. Also because of its high elevation, most of West Virginia is still undeveloped wilderness. It is a popular vacation spot for people who like to hike, boat, fish, and hunt. The state has a lot of state parks, and large national forests such as the George Washington National Forest and the Monongahela National Forest.

History

Before European settlement of the area, most of West Virginia was too rugged for the Native Americans to be interested in living there. After all, why would people live in a place where they couldn't grow any food or find many animals to hunt? However, the Shawnee, Miami, and several other tribes were able to settle in a few of the less rugged parts of West Virginia, mostly in the northern part of the state, in the Ohio River Valley.

ALL ABOUT West Virginia

CAPITAL: Charleston
LARGEST CITY: Charleston
POPULATION: 1,808,344 (2000 Census)
STATE BIRD: Cardinal
STATE TREE: Sugar Maple
STATE FLOWER: Big Laurel
STATE MOTTO: *"Montani Semper Liberi* (Mountaineers Are Always Free)"
STATEHOOD: June 20, 1863
POSTAL ABBREVIATION: WV

WORDS TO KNOW

Secede

When the voting citizens of one part of a country or a state or a county decide that they no longer want to be part of that country or state or county, they are saying that they wish to "secede" from it, or leave it. The southern states during the Civil War tried to secede from the United States and form a separate government.

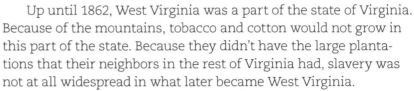

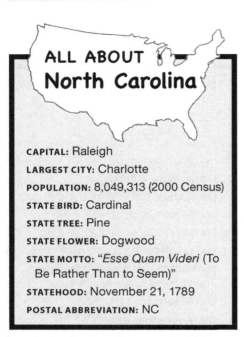

ALL ABOUT North Carolina

CAPITAL: Raleigh

LARGEST CITY: Charlotte

POPULATION: 8,049,313 (2000 Census)

STATE BIRD: Cardinal

STATE TREE: Pine

STATE FLOWER: Dogwood

STATE MOTTO: "*Esse Quam Videri* (To Be Rather Than to Seem)"

STATEHOOD: November 21, 1789

POSTAL ABBREVIATION: NC

Up until 1862, West Virginia was a part of the state of Virginia. Because of the mountains, tobacco and cotton would not grow in this part of the state. Because they didn't have the large plantations that their neighbors in the rest of Virginia had, slavery was not at all widespread in what later became West Virginia.

So when the rest of Virginia voted to secede from the Union, the counties that made up West Virginia voted to break away from Virginia! The people of West Virginia had the help of the Union Army, which protected them because they wanted to stay in the Union. Congress passed a law allowing West Virginia to enter the Union on June 20, 1863.

NORTH CAROLINA: The Tarheel State

Geography and Industry

From long, thin barrier islands in the east to the tallest mountains east of the Mississippi River to the west, North Carolina is home to a wide range of climates and terrains. Because of such barrier islands as Ocracoke and such famous capes as Cape Fear, Cape Lookout, and Cape Hatteras, North Carolina has a lot of large bays called "sounds." The most important of these are Pamlico and Albemarle Sounds, and they attract boaters, water-skiers, and fishing enthusiasts the year round. If you plan to visit North Carolina's shores, try to see places such as the Cape Hatteras National Seashore, and the Wright Brothers National Memorial at Kitty Hawk.

West of the barrier islands and the sounds lies the tidewater area. It is flat, humid, and riddled with swamps. Several large rivers run through it, including the Tar, Neuse, Cape Fear, and Roanoke rivers.

Farther west of the tidewater area is the Piedmont: rolling hills that are excellent farmland. The Piedmont rises at first gradually, then more steeply into the Blue Ridge Mountains, which are as rugged as any mountains east of the Rockies! The scenery is so breathtaking, and the climate is so mild, that western North Carolina is visited by campers and hikers year-round. North Carolina has four large national forests as well The Great Smoky Mountains

National Park, and the Appalachian Trail passes through western North Carolina, so there are plenty of places to camp, fish, or hike.

Like its neighbor Virginia, North Carolina produces a lot of tobacco, a cash crop with a long history in the state. In fact, North Carolina is the leading producer of tobacco in the world. Since smoking cigarettes in this country has declined over the past few years, farmers in North Carolina have begun to grow other crops in greater numbers. Sweet potatoes, peanuts, corn, and soybeans have been grown in North Carolina for a long time, and now they are beginning to replace tobacco in fields throughout the state.

History

Before European exploration and settlement, the largest tribes in what is now North Carolina were the Tuscarora in the central part of the state and the Cherokee in the mountain valleys of the western part of the state. The Tuscarora eventually went to war with the English colonists. The result was a disaster. After the Tuscaroras lost their fight with the colonists of North Carolina, they were forced to move all the way to western New York, where their cousins the Iroquois welcomed them as the sixth nation in their confederacy.

The Cherokees handled the advancing frontier very differently. They adopted European clothes, language, and many other customs, including their farming practices. (The Cherokees will be discussed in more detail in Chapter 4.)

You know from reading about Virginia earlier in this chapter that Jamestown was the first English settlement in North America. But, it wasn't the *first* English settlement in the New World. It was just the first permanent one! The first English colony in what is now the United States was not at Plymouth or Jamestown. It was Roanoke Colony, in what is now North Carolina.

Because it was so far away from England, Roanoke was difficult to establish, and it was hard to keep the colony supplied with food and even fresh water. This was a big problem. An expedition intended to resupply Roanoke found the colony deserted and its occupants gone without a trace and with no sign of a struggle! It seemed like the colonists had just disappeared. Carved into the

Fun Facts

THE WRIGHT BROTHERS

Kitty Hawk is the site of the first airplane flight in 1903. Two Ohio bicycle shop owners named Orville and Wilbur Wright used the strong winds of Kitty Hawk to help them get their first airplane off the ground. Today you can see the Wright Brothers' airplane at the Smithsonian Institution.

post of one of the colony's houses was a single word: CROATOAN, (which is a slight misspelling of the name of a local Indian tribe, the Croatan). Whether this was a clue about what happened to the colonists of Roanoke, no one knows for certain.

It was another sixty years before settlers from the Virginia colony moved south and began to successfully establish homes in what was then called the Carolinas (after the Latin name of the English king Charles I). The Carolina colonies were officially separated into North and South Carolina in 1712, the same year that the Tuscarora War broke out.

In 1861 North Carolina joined eleven other southern slave states (states where slavery was legal at the time) in seceding from the Union and establishing the Confederate States of America. Aside from having most of its ports captured by the blockading Union Navy, North Carolina saw little fighting during the civil war that followed secession.

In late April of 1865, the last Confederate army still in the field surrendered to Union forces in North Carolina. This occurred more than two weeks after General Robert E. Lee's main army surrendered at Appomattox in Virginia.

KENTUCKY: The Bluegrass State

Geography

If you're going to be in central and western Kentucky, don't miss the horse farms in the bluegrass region around Lexington, or the track where many of those horses race in the world-famous Kentucky Derby at Churchill Downs. Out west of the bluegrass is a region named after a kind of mint that grows there called the Pennyroyal. One sight to see in the Pennyroyal is Mammoth Cave. Mammoth Cave goes on for miles, and parts of it are open to the public.

History

Before European exploration and settlement, Kentucky was a no man's land for Native Americans. The land was fertile, and full

ALL ABOUT
Kentucky

CAPITAL: Frankfort

LARGEST CITY: Louisville

POPULATION: 4,041,769 (2000 Census)

STATE BIRD: Cardinal

STATE TREE: Kentucky Coffee Tree

STATE FLOWER: Goldenrod

STATE MOTTO: "United We Stand, Divided We Fall"

STATEHOOD: June 1, 1792

POSTAL ABBREVIATION: KY

One to Grow On

Two sisters from Louisville, Kentucky wrote a simple song in 1893.
Every single person you know can sing this song and knows all the words!
What is it? To find out, fill in all the boxes with a dot in the center.

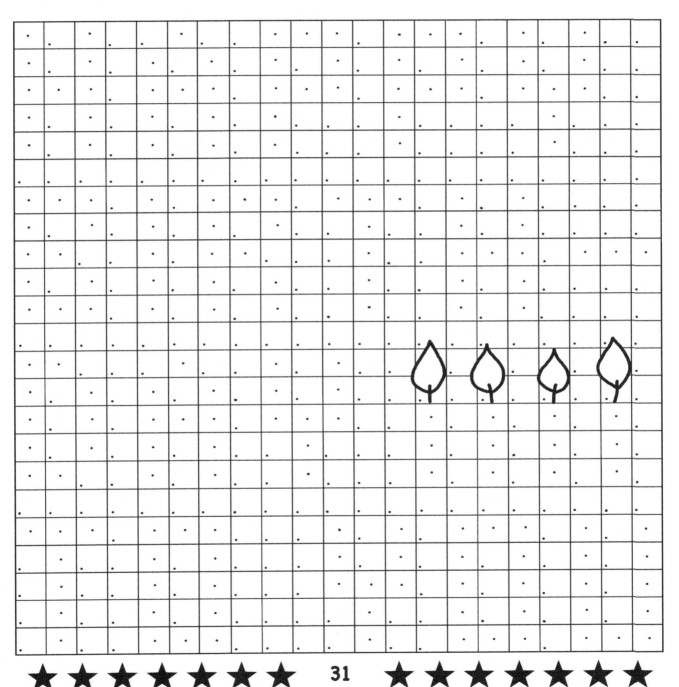

WORDS TO KNOW

Bluegrass

Bluegrass is the common name for the lawn and pasture grass in the eastern United States from Tennesse northward. Bluegrass has also come to mean the region of the United States around the Kentucky area that is known for its excellent soil, horse farms, and rolling hills of bluegrass.

of game animals. It was a great place to find food. This led to several large tribes such as the Shawnee, the Ottawa, the Delaware (who had been pushed out of the eastern colonies), the Cherokee, and the Tensa (Tennessee) fighting over these large hunting grounds. Because none of them could defeat all of their enemies, these tribes lived around Kentucky (but not in it), and ventured into it to hunt and fish, and to fight each other!

Kentucky was originally claimed by the French though they did not settle there or even enter the area. While the Native Americans ventured into Kentucky to fight each other, the French avoided the area, and instead traded furs just outside of the Kentucky border with the tribes.

After the English won Kentucky in a war with the French, their colonies on the Atlantic coast began sending settlers through the Cumberland Gap into Kentucky. The famous frontiersman Daniel Boone visited Kentucky for the first time in 1767. He founded one of the first permanent settlements in the area at Boonesboro in 1774. This wave of settlement led to savage fighting with Indian tribes living around Kentucky, especially the Shawnee.

Sitting between the Deep South and the lower states of the North, Kentucky was truly what historians call a border state. Kentucky's climate was not like that of states such as Alabama and Mississippi. In those states it was hot enough that plantation farming made money for farmers. Kentucky was too cold to grow much cotton or tobacco. Since it wasn't a good place for these crops, there wasn't as much need for slaves to work the fields in Kentucky.

But Kentucky was settled mostly by people from southern states such as Virginia (including Abraham Lincoln's grandfather, who sold his farm in Virginia to reside in Kentucky!), and in many ways was a truly southern state. So when the Civil War came, families and friendships in that state were torn apart.

Kentucky never seceded from the Union, although many Kentuckians fought on both sides of the war. The sons of a U.S. senator from Kentucky split down the middle: one fought for the North, and one fought for the South. In Kentucky the Civil War literally was a case of "brother against brother"!

A Famous Kentucky Taste

In 1930, Harland Sanders owned a gas station in Corbin, Tennessess and decided to start selling chicken cooked with his personal recipe of herbs and spices right at the station. His food quickly became popular, and the governor made him an honorary "Kentucky Colonel" six years later in! In 1952 the Colonel began opening chain restaurants. Kentucky Fried Chicken is still headquartered in Louisville, Kentucky.

TENNESSEE: The Volunteer State
Geography and Industry

Eastern Tennessee is very rugged, with a lot of forests and many narrow river valleys. Central Tennessee is like central Kentucky to the north: it is open country that has lots of bluegrass in it. Western Tennessee is some of the richest farmland in the United States. Much of the cotton grown in the United States comes from the fields of western Tennessee.

The Tennessee River flows through the central part of the state, then down into Alabama, and back north into western Tennessee, up through Kentucky, and on into the Ohio River. The Tennessee River is one of the largest and most important rivers in the south.

There is so much to see and do in Tennessee. With the Mississippi River next door, and the Tennessee River itself winding through the state, boating, water-skiing, and fishing are all very popular, to say nothing of bass fishing, which many Tennesseans take very seriously. And since Tennessee has more than twenty state parks, as well as parts of the Cherokee National Forest, the Great Smoky Mountains National Park, and the Cumberland Gap National Historical Park within its borders, there are plenty of places in Tennessee to camp and hike as well.

Tennessee has many historic places worth visiting. These include President Andrew Jackson's plantation, The Hermitage. Shiloh National Military Park marks the site of the Civil War battle of Shiloh in the west, and the Chickamauga and Chattanooga National Military Park does the same for the Chattanooga battlefield in the southeastern part of the state.

ALL ABOUT Tennessee

CAPITAL: Nashville

LARGEST CITY: Memphis

POPULATION: 5,689,283 (2000 Census)

STATE BIRD: Mockingbird

STATE TREE: Tulip Poplar

STATE FLOWER: Iris

STATE MOTTO: "Agriculture and Commerce."

STATEHOOD: June 1, 1796

POSTAL ABBREVIATION: TN

Fun Facts

THE "STATE" OF FRANKLIN

East Tennesseans formed a state government in 1784 because they felt abandoned by North Carolina. The state "existed" for four years but it was never recognized by the U.S. government.

TRY THIS!

Graceland

Have you ever heard your parents talking about the famous singer Elvis? Elvis's home is now a museum in Tennessee that's called Graceland. Make up a game with your friends about who can name the most Elvis songs. Or ask your parents to help you dig up some of their Elvis records and see if you can count how many times Elvis mentions Graceland in the lyrics.

Also, Tennessee is the home of Nashville, which is the country music capital of the world. If blues is more your thing, then Memphis, in the western part of Tennessee, might be a better place for you to visit, because Memphis is a hotbed of blues music!

History

Before the first Europeans visited Tennessee during the 1540s, tribes of Native American peoples like the Shawnee, Cherokee, and Chickasaw lived in the area. Hundreds of years earlier, the region was dominated by the Mound Builder culture. These people constructed various styles and sizes of mounds for burial, ceremonial, and residential purposes. The mounds can be found all over Tennessee.

During the American Revolution, Tennessee was part of North Carolina (just like Kentucky to the north was a county in Virginia). East Tennessee was already settled by a number of Carolinians, including a heroic Revolutionary War leader named John Sevier.

Tennessee nearly split up during the Civil War. Eastern Tennessee was mountainous and not a good place to grow plantation crops such as tobacco and cotton. Like the people in the mountains of West Virginia, the people who lived in eastern Tennessee's Great Smoky Mountains supported the Union during the war, and did not want to secede. The rest of Tennessee was plantation country, and supported slavery. Most of the people living there (aside from the slaves themselves, obviously!) wanted to secede.

It turned out to be a costly choice. Aside from Virginia, no state saw more fighting during the Civil War than Tennessee. Union troops in the western part of the state invaded the south by fighting their way along the main rivers in the state. Rivers were surrounded by valleys that made it easy for armies to move together.

Because of its position as a place from which to launch not one but two invasions of the south, getting and keeping control of Tennessee was very important to the Union during the Civil War. In fact, it was so important that in 1864, when President Lincoln was running for re-election, he took as his running mate a senator from Tennessee who had refused to give up his seat in Congress when his home state seceded.

CHAPTER 4

THE DEEP SOUTH

Swamps. Mint juleps. Moss-covered plantation houses. These are the images that come to mind when people think of the Deep South. And yet there is so much more to the Deep South than that! Florida has long beaches, a colorful Caribbean subculture, and Disney World in Orlando. South Carolina has gorgeous beaches as well, with Myrtle Beach being one of its most famous.

And the food! If you like it deep-fried, you'll like the Deep South! They even deep-fry vegetables in the Deep South (like fried okra). And then there's the barbecue, and the cornbread!

The Deep South is a place of many contrasts. It has mountains and lowlands, swamps and prairies, forests and bayous. It is also a land of large, powerful rivers such as the Mississippi, Alabama, Tennessee, and Tombigbee.

SOUTH CAROLINA: The Palmetto State
Geography and Industry

South Carolina is one of the most stereotypically "southern" of southern states. In the Palmetto State, "barbecue" is a noun as well as a verb, the weather is hot, cotton is grown all over, and plantations still dot the landscape.

The southern part of the state is covered in cypress swamps, and the northeastern part of the state has wonderful white-sand beaches, which are a year-round tourist attraction. Places such as Myrtle Beach, the Sea Islands, and the Grand Strand draw people from all over the world. So does the beautiful city of Charleston in the south, with its historic old homes, and the Fort Sumter National Monument marking where the Civil War began.

The Blue Ridge Mountains run through the northwestern part of the state, making it more rugged than the other two sections, which are coastal areas. Lots of vegetables (especially many kinds of squash) are grown in the northwestern hills of the state.

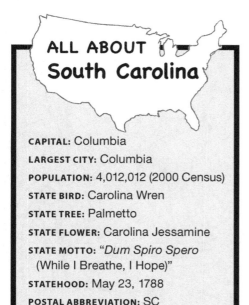

ALL ABOUT South Carolina

CAPITAL: Columbia

LARGEST CITY: Columbia

POPULATION: 4,012,012 (2000 Census)

STATE BIRD: Carolina Wren

STATE TREE: Palmetto

STATE FLOWER: Carolina Jessamine

STATE MOTTO: *"Dum Spiro Spero* (While I Breathe, I Hope)"

STATEHOOD: May 23, 1788

POSTAL ABBREVIATION: SC

Indigo (a plant that produces the blue dye of the same name) and rice have been cash crops in the Palmetto State for centuries. South Carolina is also a leader in the textile industry. This is because so much cotton is grown in the state, and because there are fast-flowing rivers such as the Edisto, Pee Dee, Santee, and Savannah that are great sources of power for cotton mills. If you're wearing a cotton shirt with a label that says Made in the U.S.A., it's pretty likely that it was made in South Carolina.

History

Before the coming of the Europeans, South Carolina was home to such powerful Native American tribes as the Catawba in the north, the Yamasee along the coast in the south, and the Cherokee in the mountainous northwest.

The first Europeans in what is now South Carolina were the members of a Spanish exploring expedition led by Lucas Vásquez de Ayllón. They occupied a site somewhere on the South Carolina coast during the year 1526. But they soon abandoned it.

By 1562, the Spanish mission system had worked its way up from Florida, and had gotten as far as what is now Charleston. The Spanish abandoned their missions in the Charleston area when the English began to colonize what they first called the Carolinas in the 1660s. This colony eventually split into two separate colonies: North and South Carolina.

The people who colonized South Carolina came from other parts of Europe besides England. There were Scots and Irish settlers, and French settlers as well. These French settlers were religious refugees called Huguenots (pronounced "HYOO-guh-nots"). While most of the people of France were Catholics, the Huguenots were Protestants, and were treated unfairly because of it. This was why many of them chose to come to the New World, where they could worship in their own way, without being bullied.

WORDS TO KNOW

Cash Crop

A cash crop is a crop that is grown strictly for the purpose of obtaining money as opposed to a crop meant to feed the farmer's family or livestock.

Fun Facts

A NEW WAY TO FIGHT

During the first years of the revolution, South Carolina did not see much action aside from hit-and-run raids by rebel units on British forces. The leaders of these rebel units became famous for their ingenuity and daring. Men such as Francis Marion (so crafty that he was nicknamed the Swamp Fox) and Thomas Sumter with their cunning, Indian-style tactics, helped change the way wars were fought.

Slavery and Secession in South Carolina

In the years between the Revolution and the Civil War, slavery became even more important in South Carolina than it had been before the United States won its independence. This was due partly because of Eli Whitney's invention of the cotton gin. Cotton became very important to South Carolina, and its textile industry boomed. That meant more cotton had to be grown. The fastest way to do that was to get more slaves, and put them to work planting and picking cotton, which led to acquiring more slaves and planting more land with cotton, and so on.

This made South Carolina politicians and property owners resist other peoples' attempts to free the slaves and to get rid of plantation life completely. In the minds of these South Carolinians, slavery stopped being a "necessary evil," and became a positive force for southern society.

South Carolina politicians wanted to see the South's way of life protected, and for them, that meant no limits on slavery in America. During a speech he gave in June of 1858, Abraham Lincoln declared, "[a] house divided against itself cannot stand. I do not believe this government can endure permanently half-slave and half-free." In 1860, Lincoln was elected president and South Carolina's leaders were so worried that he would abolish slavery throughout the country that they voted to leave the Union. They ordered the state's militia to seize federal forts and armories within South Carolina's borders.

One such federal fort was Fort Sumter, which protected the Charleston harbor. When rebel gunners fired their cannons at the fort in an effort to get its commander to surrender, the Civil War began. The date was April 12, 1861.

As it turned out, there was very little fighting in South Carolina during the four-year struggle that followed. Aside from the Union navy occupying the Sea Islands as part of a blockade of all southern ports, South Carolina saw no major military activity within its borders until the very end of the war.

GEORGIA: The Peach State

Geography and Industry

The southern tip of the Blue Ridge Mountains rises in Georgia's northwestern sector, and forms one of the state's three geographic regions. These mountains are part of the Appalachian chain, and run all the way north into West Virginia!

Georgia's two other regions are the hilly Piedmont, which slopes down from the Blue Ridge across the central part of the state, and the southeastern coastal plain, which includes the large Okefenokee Swamp. Georgia also shares the Sea Islands with South Carolina, its neighbor to the north.

Georgia's rivers help form most of its borders with the states that surround it. The Savannah River runs along Georgia's border with South Carolina. The Chattahoochie in the west forms part of Georgia's boundary with Alabama, and the St. Mary's in the south is the marker for part of the Georgia-Florida border.

Georgia has the southern end of the Appalachian Trail in its northwestern section, and as a result, has many places within its borders to hike and camp. Many Georgians also love to hunt and fish. Along Georgia's coastline, surf fishing is incredibly popular. Places such as Warm Springs, the Sea Islands, and the Civil War battlefield national monuments at Chickamauga and Kennesaw Mountain draw millions of tourists every year.

Cotton used to be the "king" crop in Georgia, but that hasn't been true for decades. These days, the top products are peanuts, lumber, tobacco, and corn. The state is covered in pine forests, and because of its warm climate and long growing season, these trees can be grown quickly and harvested more often than in other timber-producing states.

History

Did you know that Georgia began as a prison? It's true! When Georgia was founded as a British royal colony in 1733, it was

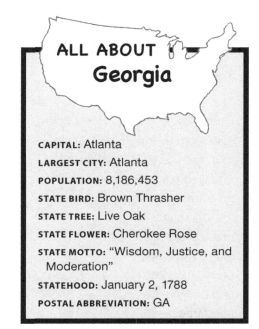

ALL ABOUT Georgia

CAPITAL: Atlanta
LARGEST CITY: Atlanta
POPULATION: 8,186,453
STATE BIRD: Brown Thrasher
STATE TREE: Live Oak
STATE FLOWER: Cherokee Rose
STATE MOTTO: "Wisdom, Justice, and Moderation"
STATEHOOD: January 2, 1788
POSTAL ABBREVIATION: GA

Fun Facts

PEANUTS

Do you like peanuts? If you do, odds are that the ones you've eaten came from Georgia. Georgia is the country's largest producer of peanuts. Former president (and Georgia resident) Jimmy Carter started out as a peanut farmer.

WORDS TO KNOW

The Trail of Tears

The trail of tears was a 116-day journey of several thousand Cherokees from their homes in Georgia to a reservation in Oklahoma. The Georgia state government forced the Cherokees to make this trip. The journey was so poorly planned and badly managed that nearly 4,000 Cherokees died on the trip.

illegal to owe money that you couldn't pay. People often went to jail until they could pay their debts. Georgia's founder James Oglethorpe thought that one way to help people in this position was to offer to send them to a colony in America, rather than send them to a jail in England, where they couldn't pay off their debt because they weren't free to work. And so Georgia (named for George II, the English king at the time) was born.

Before European settlement, Native American tribes such as the Cherokee (who lived in the Blue Ridge mountains of the northwest) and the Muskogean-speaking Creek (who lived in the river valleys of the west) lived in Georgia. Other, smaller Muskogean-speaking tribes lived along Georgia's swampy southeastern coast.

As the Georgia frontier advanced inland, it ran into the lands of the Cherokees beginning shortly before the American Revolution. At first the Cherokee fought the settlers moving into their land. Then they had a brilliant idea.

The Cherokee began to adopt the ways of the European settlers. They dressed like their white neighbors, settled down to raise cotton and tobacco, even owned black slaves and used them for labor on Cherokee plantations!

This accommodation of American settlers did not help the Cherokee in the long run, though. By the early 1830s, gold had been discovered on Cherokee land, and most of them were forced to give up their homes in Georgia and move west to a reservation set aside for them in distant Oklahoma.

Whereas Georgia escaped the American Revolution without having a major battle fought within its borders, the Civil War that came ninety years later utterly destroyed most of the property in the state. Union general William Tecumseh Sherman led a large army southeast from Tennessee and through the heart of Georgia, all the way to the sea. Sherman's troops seized all farm supplies (including grain) and most of the farm animals of the people who lived in their path.

What they didn't take, Sherman's army burned. This included the large and prosperous city of Atlanta. Sherman became so hated in Georgia that for generations after the war, if you toasted General Sherman anywhere in Georgia, you were literally asking for a fight!

Pickles?

Of all the states, Georgia is the biggest producer of the "three Ps." Follow the directions below to cross items out of the grid. When you are done, you will know what the three Ps are!

POMEGRANATES	PEAS	PAPAYAS
PARSNIPS	PEANUTS	PEARS
PECANS	PENCILS	PEPPERS
PALMETTOS	PIMENTOS	PUMPKINS
PASTA	PUZZLES	PRETZELS
POPCORN	PORK	PINEAPPLES
PAPRIKA	PENNIES	PLOWS
PATIOS	POTATOES	PEACHES
PICKLES	PUDDING	PASTRIES
PLUMS	PETUNIAS	PANCAKES

Cross out all items that...

...are not edible

...have double letters

...start with PA

...have the letter K

...are less than 6 letters

...are more than 7 letters

...have the letter O

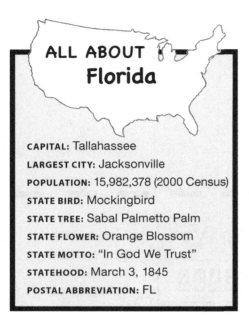

ALL ABOUT Florida

CAPITAL: Tallahassee

LARGEST CITY: Jacksonville

POPULATION: 15,982,378 (2000 Census)

STATE BIRD: Mockingbird

STATE TREE: Sabal Palmetto Palm

STATE FLOWER: Orange Blossom

STATE MOTTO: "In God We Trust"

STATEHOOD: March 3, 1845

POSTAL ABBREVIATION: FL

Fun Facts

ST. AUGUSTINE

You know about Jamestown in Virginia, and about Plymouth in Massachusetts, but do you know about St. Augustine in Florida? It is the oldest city in North America. Spanish settlers established it in 1565, almost fifty years before Jamestown!

FLORIDA: The Sunshine State

Geography and Industry

Florida is mostly a giant peninsula surrounded on three sides by salt water, and is possibly the flattest state in the Union. It's true! Florida is even flatter than such plains states as Kansas and Nebraska. It's also a huge state, one of the largest in the country.

Have you ever visited a wetland? Well, Florida is home to the Everglades, which is a unique type of country: it is part swamp and part cypress forest, and all wetland. In fact, it's one of the largest wetlands in the world. Like many other things in Florida, the Everglades country is huge. It covers a lot of the southern tip of the state, and much of it lies within the Everglades National Park.

In the north, Florida is covered by a combination of pine and palmetto forests. There are many swamps in the northwestern part of the state as well, in addition to such large rivers as the Perdido River and the St. Mary's River. On Florida's east coast there are a lot of barrier islands: long, thin islands that protect the coastline from the tides, and naturally prevent erosion.

Speaking of islands, don't forget the Florida Keys. They are a chain of islands that extend southwestward from the southern tip of Florida for hundreds of miles out into the Gulf of Mexico. And they even have a highway that runs between them!

History

Native Americans have been active in Florida for at least the past 10,000 years. When Juan Ponce de Leon explored Florida for Spain in 1519, there were thousands and thousands of Native Americans (mostly members of a language group called the Apalachee) living there. We know very little about these people, because so many died after the explorers came into their land. The Spaniards who followed Ponce de Leon to Florida in the decades afterward brought European diseases like smallpox, influenza, and whooping cough that made the Indians sick enough to die. On top of that, the Spanish explorers who came to Florida, looking for the same gold and silver they had found in South America and Mexico, tried to enslave the native population, killing many of them outright in the

struggle. It was a horrible time to be a Native American in Florida!

In 1819, Spain sold Florida to the United States for $5,000,000. Why? First, the Spanish military had been weakened by recent wars in Europe. The Spanish government was afraid that the United States would simply move in and take Florida from Spain without Spain receiving anything in return. Second, at about this time, an American army under the command of General Andrew Jackson chased Seminole Indians from southern Georgia into Florida. The Spanish were not able to stop Jackson and his militia. This incident convinced the Spanish that if they didn't sell Florida to the United States, they would soon lose it anyway.

By 1845 Florida had enough American citizens living in its borders to become a state. Just sixteen years later, Florida sided with the other southern states, and helped found the Confederacy.

Florida saw almost no fighting during the Civil War. The Union Navy did seize a few strategic coastal towns, though. After the Civil War, Florida experienced a huge real estate boom. People made millions buying and selling Florida property.

Real estate is still an important and money-making industry in Florida even today. But can you guess what Florida's most important industry is today? Here's a hint: "I'm going to Disney World!" That's right, tourism is the answer. Every year, millions of people from all over the world visit Florida on vacation, and not just to see Disney World. They also visit Miami's restaurants and shops, take boat cruises that begin in Jacksonville, and enjoy the miles and miles of beaches all along Florida's coastline.

WORDS TO KNOW

Seminole

Seminoles are members of the Creek Nation of Indians. Their name means "separators," because they left the Creek homeland in Alabama and moved south, into Florida, during the eighteenth century. From Florida, the Seminoles encouraged runaway slaves and members of other tribes to join them and intermarry with them.

ALABAMA: The Yellowhammer State
Geography and Industry

Alabama has a few mountains in the northeast (it's part of the Cumberland Plateau). Aside from them, the state is very flat. The Piedmont section in the middle part of the state rolls down to the coastal plain, which lies around the huge harbor of Mobile Bay. The Tennessee River winds through Alabama's northern section, then back into Tennessee. And the Alabama and Tombigbee rivers flow through the central section and drain into the Gulf of Mexico in

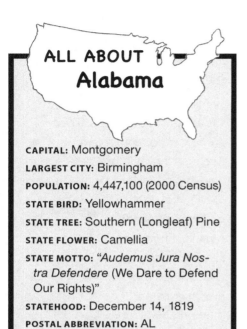

ALL ABOUT Alabama

CAPITAL: Montgomery

LARGEST CITY: Birmingham

POPULATION: 4,447,100 (2000 Census)

STATE BIRD: Yellowhammer

STATE TREE: Southern (Longleaf) Pine

STATE FLOWER: Camellia

STATE MOTTO: *"Audemus Jura Nostra Defendere (We Dare to Defend Our Rights)"*

STATEHOOD: December 14, 1819

POSTAL ABBREVIATION: AL

Fun Facts

HOME OF THE CONFEDERATE CAPITAL

Did you know that Richmond, Virginia, was not the original capital of the Confederate States of America? Because Virginia did not secede from the Union until many months after the states of the Deep South did, the capital was originally located in Montgomery, Alabama.

the south. These large, navigable river systems are popular year-round with boaters and fishermen.

Alabama is the site of some of the largest caves in the United States as well. One particular set, which was lived in continually by Native Americans for thousands of years, can be found at Russell Cave National Monument. Another popular Alabama tourist attraction is Mound State Monument, where early Native American burial mounds have been preserved.

As with its neighbors Georgia and Mississippi, cotton used to be the only real product of Alabama. These days manufacturing is very important in this state, where power is cheap and plentiful because of the hydroelectric dams on the Tennessee River. Roaster chickens are also raised in Alabama (as they are in Mississippi).

History

Before European settlement, Alabama was home to many large Native American tribes. The Cherokee lived in the northeast, the Creek in the southeast, the Choctaw in the southwest, and the Chickasaw in the northwest. All of the tribes except for the Cherokee spoke dialects of the Muskogean language, and because of Alabama's fertile black soil and year-round warm weather, they were all farmers.

The Spanish explored Alabama first. Cabeza de Vaca visited the region in 1528, and Hernando de Soto in 1540. De Soto's men were terribly destructive. They fought many of the local tribes and burned many native towns.

The French were the first Europeans to permanently settle in the region. They established a fur-trading post in Mobile Bay in 1702. For the next century, the fur trade was the major reason for European settlement in the region.

By the early 1800s, American settlers from Tennessee and Georgia had begun to plant cotton in Alabama, and the numbers of the Americans in the region boomed. Crowded westward by American settlement, the Creek nation went to war to protect their lands. American militia troops under the command of Tennessee general Andrew Jackson defeated the Creek confederacy at the battle of Horseshoe Bend in 1814. As a result, the Creeks gave up their lands, and agreed to be moved to what is now Oklahoma. The Choctaw and Chickasaw soon followed them there.

When the Civil War broke out in 1861, few southern states were as ready for a fight as Alabama. It was among the first states to follow South Carolina's example and secede from the Union. Although (like South Carolina) Alabama provided many soldiers for the southern cause during the war, it saw very little fighting (also like South Carolina). The exception to this was the huge naval battle at Mobile Bay in 1864. The Union won it, and continued to blockade the South's trade with Europe.

MISSISSIPPI: The Magnolia State
Geography and Industry

Mississippi has many different types of land within its borders. In the northern part of the state there are hills and river valleys cut by small, fast-flowing rivers. The southern part is taken up mostly by the broad floodplain of the Mississippi River. This plain is called the Mississippi Delta, and runs between the mouth of the Mississippi River in the west and that of the Yazoo River in the east.

After Eli Whitney invented the cotton gin and made cotton such an important crop, places like Mississippi became very important centers of the growth of cotton. Although not as important as it once was, cotton is still grown all over Mississippi's delta region today. With cotton not being grown so much anymore, a lot of Mississippi's rich farmland is currently devoted to cattle-ranching and chicken-raising. If you've ever had roaster chicken, it probably came from Mississippi.

History

Before European exploration and settlement, Mississippi was home to large tribes of Native Americans such as the Choctaw, Chickasaw, and Natchez. The Spaniards visited the region first, and Hernando de Soto's men discovered the Mississippi River in 1541.

The French, in 1699, established a trading post on the coast, near Biloxi. Over the next century, the area changed hands between the

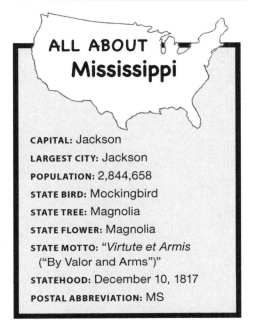

ALL ABOUT Mississippi

CAPITAL: Jackson
LARGEST CITY: Jackson
POPULATION: 2,844,658
STATE BIRD: Mockingbird
STATE TREE: Magnolia
STATE FLOWER: Magnolia
STATE MOTTO: *"Virtute et Armis* ("By Valor and Arms")"
STATEHOOD: December 10, 1817
POSTAL ABBREVIATION: MS

Delta

A delta takes its name from the Greek letter *delta*, which is triangular in shape. Greek visitors to the Nile River noticed that the river dumped a lot of the soil it carried from upstream at its mouth, that this soil was excellent for farming, and that the shape of the river's floodplain was roughly triangular in shape. This is why the Greeks called the area the delta.

French, Spanish, and English numerous times. In the treaty that ended the American Revolution, the English ceded most of what is now Mississippi to the United States. The southern part came to the United States as part of the Louisiana Purchase in 1803.

Just as they did in Alabama, by the 1820s, cotton-growing American settlers displaced the Native American population, and began to take the rich farmland in the delta. By the time the Civil War began in 1861, Mississippi was a cotton empire. Its plantation owners made millions from the British demand for the crop, and slavery flourished.

As a result, the state joined the other states of the Deep South in seceding from the Union. In fact, Mississippi also supplied the Confederacy with its first and only president: former Mississippi senator and U.S. Secretary of War, Jefferson Davis.

Like Virginia and Georgia in the east, Mississippi was a battleground state during the Civil War. The important battles of Shiloh, Jackson, and Vicksburg were all fought in Mississippi. The loss of Vicksburg to the Union forces is considered by many historians to be the turning point in the American Civil War.

Where are my glasses?

Start in one of the corners and read the letters in order around the grid and into the middle. You must find which corner to start, and in which direction to read! When you are finished, you will have the silly answer to this riddle: Why is Mississippi such an unusual state?

S	F	O	U	R	E	Y	E	S
A	A	N'T	S	E	E	!	A
H	C	L	L	I	T	S	D	N
T	I	E	S	U	A	C	E	B

The Midwestern states might also be called the Great Lakes states, because each of them (even the mostly land-locked Indiana) at least partially borders the Great Lakes. Such large continental rivers as the Ohio and the Mississippi are also important in tying the states of this region together.

Most of the states of the Midwest are part of what is now known as the Rust Belt, as well. This is a part of the country that built up huge manufacturing plants because of its closeness to coal and oil deposits, its central location, and its good transportation routes to other parts of the country (first by riverboat, then by railroad) and to the world.

Several of the cities in this section of the country have been very important to the development of American industry, including Detroit, Cleveland, Milwaukee, and especially Chicago. The Midwest region of the country ties the other sections together.

OHIO: The Buckeye State

Geography

Ohio is bordered to the south by the river for which it is named. To the north lies Lake Erie. Ohio is mostly flat, with some rolling hills in the southeastern part of the state. Before European settlement, Ohio was a big, unbroken hardwood forest. Most of that huge forest is gone now, replaced by some of the richest farmland in the country. Wheat is grown in Ohio, nearly as much as is grown in the plains states!

In the Ohio River Valley, you can find a number of large earthen mounds. These were left by a group of Native Americans that archaeologists call the Hopewell civilization. Other people refer to these people as the Mound Builders. This civilization, which disappeared hundreds of years before European exploration of the region, built mounds that measure as high as sixty-five feet off the ground, and in some places they cover

ALL ABOUT
Ohio

CAPITAL: Columbus
LARGEST CITY: Columbus
POPULATION: 11,353,140 (2000 Census)
STATE BIRD: Cardinal
STATE TREE: Buckeye
STATE FLOWER: Scarlet Carnation
STATE MOTTO: "With God, All Things Are Possible"
STATEHOOD: March 1, 1803
POSTAL ABBREVIATION: OH

acres of ground! Some of these mounds are circular; others are in the shape of animals such as snakes. You can find many of these interesting mounds in the Hopewell Culture National Historical Park.

History

After the end of the Hopewell civilization, other tribes entered the Ohio country and prospered there. Tribes such as the Miami, the Shawnee, and the Erie settled in the region. During the seventeenth century, the Erie fought a long war with the Seneca, a member tribe of the Iroquois confederacy, which lived in western New York. The two tribes fought over control of the fur trade in the Ohio region. The Erie lost, and were absorbed by the Seneca, who took over the Erie hunting grounds as their own.

During the eighteenth century, most of the tribes in the Ohio country sided with the French in a series of wars with the English. Because the French had claimed all of the lands drained by the waters that flowed out of the mouth of the Mississippi and into the Gulf of Mexico, they had a claim to the Ohio country as well, because the Ohio River flows into the Mississippi.

When the French lost their lands in North America as part of the treaty that ended the Seven Years' War (1756–1763), many of the Native Americans in the Ohio Valley joined in what later became known as Pontiac's Rebellion. This wave of violence led to the eventual removal of all Native American tribes to west of the Mississippi River.

After the American Revolution, the British ceded Ohio to the United States as part of the Old Northwest Territory. Ohio became its own territory in 1799, and a state in 1803.

Shortly after Ohio became a state, it became a battleground of the War of 1812, which the young United States fought with Great Britain. One of the most important battles of this war was an American naval victory over the British on Lake Erie, within sight of the Ohio shore.

WORDS TO KNOW

Drain

When geographers use this term they are usually using it as a verb, to explain which rivers and streams "drain" a region. In other words, saying that a river "drains" a region means that the water that flows out of the area goes by way of this river (and its tributary streams) to the ocean.

Fun Facts

OHIO: THE MOTHER OF PRESIDENTS!

Ohio has supplied more presidents to our country than any other state, eight presidents in all! Aside from William Henry Harrison (who was born in Virginia, and moved to Ohio when it was still a territory), all of these presidents were born and raised in Ohio: Ulysses S. Grant, Rutherford B. Hayes, James A. Garfield, Benjamin Harrison, William McKinley, William Howard Taft, and Warren G. Harding.

Industry in Ohio

Ohio has changed a lot in the 200 years since it became a state. Because it had a lot of natural resources like oil, coal, and natural gas, Ohio was a natural choice for people who were looking for places to build factories to produce goods like cloth. Later, as the Industrial Revolution helped make it easier to produce high-grade steel products, Ohio's coal deposits were one reason that the state became a center of steel production in the United States.

The other reason Ohio became so important in industry was its water access to other markets. In the southern part of the state, the mighty Ohio River fed into the Mississippi, and out of the Gulf of Mexico and to foreign markets. In the north there was Lake Erie, which fed eventually into the St. Lawrence River, and again, out to sea, and to foreign markets in places such as England, which was a large market for American steel during the nineteenth century.

As a result of this, Ohio became a very important state in the Union, before, during, and after the Civil War. Many of America's military and political leaders came from Ohio during this century, including Union generals Ulysses S. Grant and William Tecumseh Sherman, and a number of U.S. presidents.

Important Ohioans

There are many great explorers among those Ohioans who have gone on to national and international fame. These include John Wesley Powell, who explored the Grand Canyon in the late nineteenth century, and Annie Oakley, the great American sharpshooter.

Then, of course, there are the Wright Brothers, who invented the airplane in 1903. They owned a bicycle shop in Dayton, Ohio, even though they are remembered for their flights at Kitty Hawk in North Carolina. Because of the contributions of the Wright Brothers, we have the later accomplishments of John Glenn, one of America's first astronauts (and later a U.S.

senator from Ohio), and Neil Armstrong, another American astronaut and the first man to walk on the moon (in 1969). Other great Ohioans include Daniel C. Beard, who founded the Boy Scouts of America, and A.B. Graham, who founded the 4-H club movement.

Get in Shape

Ohio's flag is unique among the 50 states. Why?

Connect the dots, and break the "Vowel Switch" Code to find out!

1.
•6

•2

Tha stuta flug if Ihei es treungolur, weth twi pientad tuels.

3.

•4

5•

ALL ABOUT Indiana

CAPITAL: Indianapolis

LARGEST CITY: Indianapolis

POPULATION: 6,080,485 (2000 Census)

STATE BIRD: Cardinal

STATE TREE: Tulip Poplar

STATE FLOWER: Peony

STATE MOTTO: "The Crossroads of America"

STATEHOOD: December 11, 1816

POSTAL ABBREVIATION: IN

Fun Facts

INDIANA LIMESTONE

The majority of the limestone used in buildings in this country comes from southern Indiana.

INDIANA: The Hoosier State

Geography and Industry

Indiana is right in the middle of both the Midwest and the United States itself. In fact, north Indiana is one of the most frequently crossed parts of the country because of its closeness to the transportation hub in the city of Chicago in the neighboring state of Illinois. More planes, trains, trucks, and cars cross northern Indiana than most other parts of the United States combined.

Northern and central Indiana are pretty flat, and ideal farmland. In fact, even though manufacturing is Indiana's biggest type of industry, 75 percent of the state is still farmland. Most of the available land is used to grow wheat, corn, soybeans, and hay. Another important Indiana crop is popcorn! Nearly half of the popcorn eaten in America is grown and packaged in Indiana. After all, Orville Redenbacher was an Indiana native.

Northwestern Indiana has a lot of heavy industry (mostly things like steel production), again because it is so close to Chicago. Southern Indiana is made up mostly of rolling limestone hills, in which groundwater has bored out immense underground caves. The major rivers in Indiana include the Ohio (which marks Indiana's southern border), the Wabash, and the Indiana.

History

The Mound Builders discussed in the section on Ohio also lived and built monuments in Indiana. After the decline of their civilization, Native American tribes such as the Shawnee, Miami, Wyandot, and Delaware (who had been pushed west first from Pennsylvania, then from Ohio by European settlement) lived in what is now Indiana.

These tribes all sided with the British during the American Revolution, and continued to fight against the United States even afterward, because they were trying to keep American set-

tlers off of their land. One of their leaders was a Shawnee Chief named Tecumseh. He was respected on both sides of the conflict for his bravery and his honesty. Tecumseh tried to unite the tribes of the Ohio Valley with other tribes west of the Appalachian Mountains, such as the Creeks and Cherokees in the south. He wanted to get these tribes to band together to keep the whites out of the lands west of the mountains.

While Tecumseh was away in the south trying to persuade the Creeks to join his confederacy, his followers fought a battle with American soldiers under the command of General (and future president) William Henry Harrison. This battle took place on November 7, 1811, on the banks of Tippecanoe Creek.

Although it was pretty much a draw, this battle made a name for Harrison, who made a political career of the event. He ran for the presidency nearly thirty years later with the campaign slogan "Tippecanoe and Tyler Too!" (John Tyler of Virginia was his running mate.)

Tecumseh sided with the British during the War of 1812. He was later killed in what is now Ontario, Canada, at the Battle of the Thames. When he died, Native American resistance to white settlement in Indiana collapsed, and most of the remaining Native American tribes in the area were relocated by the U.S. government to lands west of the Mississippi River.

TRY THIS!

Ancient Native American Food: Popcorn

Did you know that Native Americans had popcorn as part of their daily diet nearly 80,000 years ago? It's true! In fact, there was a bag of popcorn brought to the first Thanksgiving. This led to the first American cold cereal: popcorn with milk poured over it, served at breakfast. If you'd like to try an early American favorite pour some milk over your plain popcorn. It may not be sweet like today's cereals but you'll be able to taste how cereal began!

Crossing Indiana

Indiana has more interstate highways per square mile than any other state. Maybe that's why its state motto is "The crossroads of America"!

See if you can find the one route that ENTERs and LEAVEs Indiana. You can travel over and under on the roads, but must stop at road blocks or dead ends!

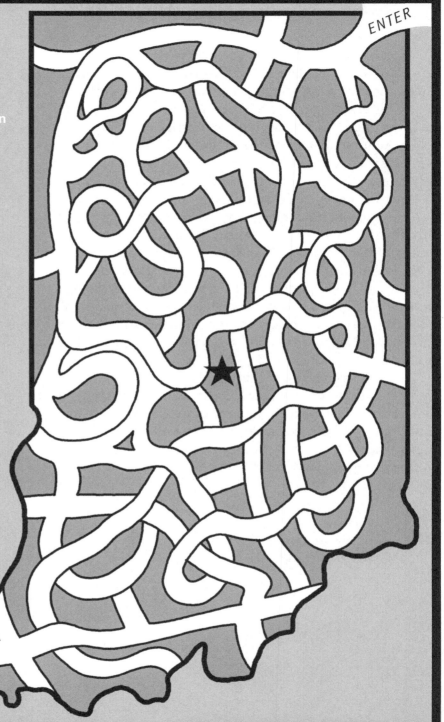

ENTER

LEAVE

ILLINOIS: The Prairie State

Geography and Industry

Illinois gets its name from the large rolling prairies that cover the state. As with most of the Midwest, there are no mountains to speak of in Illinois. The state is both bordered and affected by a number of large rivers: the Mississippi in the west, the Ohio and Wabash in the southeast, and the Illinois River, the largest river in the state, which runs across Illinois to drain into the Mississippi itself.

Although noted for its large prairies, the state has a number of hardwood forests in various portions of it, including the vast tracts to be found in the Shawnee National Forest. Places like the Cahokia Mounds have remnants of large burial mounds left behind by the ancient Mississippian civilization, too.

Illinois is located close to the geographic center of the country, and as a result, its largest city, Chicago, is the central transportation hub in the United States. Transcontinental flights routinely stop over in Chicago's O'Hare Airport, one of the world's largest. Also, the city has been the eastern endpoint of a number of national railroads for over a century. Freight that gets shipped through Chicago frequently gets shifted from the railroad to a container ship, which in turn can take it out of the Great Lakes, through the St. Lawrence Seaway to parts of the East Coast or overseas markets.

History

Well before the arrival of European explorers in the region, a mound-building Native American civilization known today as the Mississippian culture had a huge presence in what is now Illinois. The ruins of this culture can still be viewed at places such as Cahokia, in the southern part of the state. At one point Cahokia was home to nearly 40,000 people and the site of a large earthen mound that stood 100 feet high and nearly 1,000 feet long. The Mississippian culture declined because of

ALL ABOUT Illinois

CAPITAL: Springfield
LARGEST CITY: Chicago
POPULATION: 12,419,293 (2000 Census)
STATE BIRD: Cardinal
STATE TREE: White Oak
STATE FLOWER: Native Violet
STATE MOTTO: "State Sovereignty, National Union"
STATEHOOD: December 3, 1818
POSTAL ABBREVIATION: IL

WORDS TO KNOW

Prairie

The word prairie comes from the French word for "meadow" and refers to a type of landscape that contains mostly grasses and herbs and a few trees. Prairies tend to have a moderate or temperate climate.

 **55**

food shortages and warfare sometime between 1250 and 1400 A.D.

After the Mississippian culture fell apart, Algonquian-speaking tribes such as the Winnebago, the Illini, and the Sauk and Fox moved in to the area, living and farming in the state's large river valleys. When the Europeans came, they were initially French and mostly fur traders. In time, they lost the land to the English, who gave up the area to the United States as part of the treaty ending the American Revolution.

As a result of the Black Hawk War of 1832, the U.S. government "removed" the Native Americans living in this area to lands across the Mississippi River. The Illinois country began to rapidly fill up with people interested in farming the region's rich black soil. To this day, Illinois produces huge quantities of crops such as wheat, soybeans, corn, and sorghum, in addition to livestock such as cattle and hogs. Because of its location and the availability of railroads to bring cattle and hogs from rural Illinois and such plains states as Kansas and Nebraska, Chicago also quickly became the center of the meat-packing industry.

After the Civil War, manufacturing in Illinois boomed. Because ironmongers had figured out how to make high-grade steel in large quantities, Chicago quickly got something it hadn't had before: a view! Chicago was the site of a massive explosion of skyscraper building during the decades right before the turn of the nineteenth century.

Because of both its booming manufacturing base and its central location in the United States, Chicago also became the catalog sales capital of the world in the late nineteenth century. Sears, Roebuck & Company (among many other catalog sales businesses) started out as a catalog store based in Chicago. In other words, you could order goods from it to be delivered anywhere that had postal service, but you couldn't go to the store, because there was no store to go to, only a supply center in Chicago.

Fun Facts

BUY YOUR HOUSE FROM A CATALOG!

At one time, there didn't seem to be anything a person couldn't buy from a Sears catalog, including a house! Beginning in 1908, Sears offered to ship a customer a house ready to be assembled for anywhere from $100 to just over $600, depending on what kind of house the buyer wanted. Sears sold about 100,000 of these houses until it discontinued the program in 1940.

MICHIGAN: The Wolverine State

Geography and Industry

Michigan is one of the most oddly and interestingly shaped states in the union. It is really nothing more than two peninsulas that are surrounded by a lot of lake water and not physically connected to each other at all! These two peninsulas are called the Lower Peninsula and the Upper Peninsula, respectively.

The Lower Peninsula is roughly hand-shaped, and juts out into two of the Great Lakes (Michigan and Huron). The majority of Michigan's population lives in this peninsula. Michigan's largest city, Detroit, is near the "thumb" of the hand-shaped peninsula. The Lower Peninsula is mostly lowland forest and rolling hills.

Michigan's Upper Peninsula is northwest of the Lower Peninsula and across Lake Michigan from it. It extends eastward from northeastern Wisconsin, with Lake Superior to the north and Lake Michigan to the south. Less than ten percent of Michigan's population lives here. It has lots of forest land, and the western portion is pretty rugged. These mountains have lots of copper and iron deposits. People come from all over the Northeast to ski in Michigan's western mountains, and to summer on its cool and temperate northern Lake Superior shore.

Most of Michigan's economy for the past century has been tied to Detroit's massive auto industry. As American car makers have lost their foremost position as makers of cars, the entire state has suffered. The last couple of decades in particular have been tough times in Detroit.

History

Michigan, before European exploration and settlement, was inhabited by Algonquin-speaking tribes of Native Americans such as the Chippewa, Ojibwa, Ottawa, Mingoes, and Potawatomi. French explorers and fur traders visited Michigan beginning in the seventeenth century. They founded trading posts at

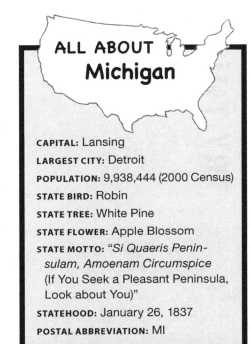

ALL ABOUT Michigan

CAPITAL: Lansing
LARGEST CITY: Detroit
POPULATION: 9,938,444 (2000 Census)
STATE BIRD: Robin
STATE TREE: White Pine
STATE FLOWER: Apple Blossom
STATE MOTTO: "*Si Quaeris Peninsulam, Amoenam Circumspice* (If You Seek a Pleasant Peninsula, Look about You)"
STATEHOOD: January 26, 1837
POSTAL ABBREVIATION: MI

TRY THIS!

Michigan: The "Hand" State

Michigan's Lower Peninsula is shaped like a hand. You can locate places in the state by looking at your left hand with the palm down, the thumb extended out a bit, and the fingers extended outward. For example, Chicago, Illinois would be placed on the left part of your wrist and Detroit would be near your thumb. Give this a try and see what other sorts of "hand directions" you can come up with!

such spots as Detroit and Michilimackinac. Detroit in particular became an important French fort, because it commanded access to the upper Great Lakes, with its site on the strategic Detroit River.

When the French lost all of their holdings to the British in 1763, Michigan became a British possession for just over twenty years. In 1783, it changed hands again, going to the Americans in the Treaty of Paris, which ended the American Revolution. For a time Michigan was part of the Old Northwest Territory, then of the Ohio Territory, then of the Indiana Territory.

When Michigan was ready to become a state itself, it got into a border dispute with neighboring Ohio. This dispute was called the Toledo War, because the site of what is now Toledo, Ohio, at the southwestern end of Lake Erie, was smack in the middle of the disputed territory. Ohio eventually won the "war" (which had only one injury and no deaths), and claimed Toledo as its prize. As compensation for losing the Toledo corridor, the federal government gave the entire Upper Peninsula over to Michigan when it became a state, in early 1837.

WISCONSIN: The Badger State
Geography and Industry

While its neighbor Minnesota is often called the Land of 10,000 Lakes, Wisconsin could easily be called the State Next Door, Which Has 8,500 Lakes. Much of northern Wisconsin is taken up by the same sorts of moraine lakes that dot neighboring Minnesota. These lakes range from huge (Lake Winnebago) to some that are small enough to be nothing more than ponds. And yet there are thousands of them!

These lakes aren't the only examples of glacial sculpting of Wisconsin's countryside. The Wisconsin Dells are another example. This rock formation is a deep canyon, about five miles in length, along the Wisconsin River. The Dells were dug out of very old sandstone by an advancing glacier during the last ice age.

Water is an important factor in Wisconsin life. Not only does it fill Wisconsin's many lakes, it also forms most of Wisconsin's borders: to the east, there's Lake Michigan, and to the north there's Lake Superior. The Mississippi River runs along Wisconsin's western edge, forming a natural border between Wisconsin and its neighbors Minnesota and Iowa. The Wisconsin River runs south through much of the state, then turns west just north of the state's capital city of Madison and runs into the Mississippi.

Wisconsin is still mostly farmland. It is a dairy state. Its farms produce large amounts of milk, cheese, and cream for coffee, tea, and (of course) ice cream! The state is also an important producer of potatoes, hay, alfalfa, apples, and the largest producer of cranberries in the United States.

Timber products have always been an important export of Wisconsin's forests, especially in northern Wisconsin. Also in the north, the Gogebic Range of mountains is a source of copper and iron. Lead is widely mined in southern Wisconsin, and has been for centuries.

History

Some of the earliest inhabitants of what is now Wisconsin were the mound builders of what we now call the Mississippian culture. They built and farmed in the region for around 1,000 years, disappearing around 1500. The Native American tribes who lived in Wisconsin when the first European explorers arrived included the Menominee, the Sauk and Fox, the Winnebago, the Kickapoo, and the Sioux. Just about the time the first explorers and fur traders arrived in the area, these tribes were already being pushed out of Wisconsin by eastern tribes such as the Huron, the Ottawa, and Ojibwa, who had in their turn been pushed westward by European settlement farther east.

The French originally claimed Wisconsin as part of their North American possessions. They established their first trading posts in the area of Green Bay during the 1660s. For the next century the French conducted a thriving fur trade with most of

ALL ABOUT Wisconsin

CAPITAL: Madison
LARGEST CITY: Milwaukee
POPULATION: 5,363,675 (2000 Census)
STATE BIRD: Robin
STATE TREE: Sugar Maple
STATE FLOWER: Wood Violet
STATE MOTTO: "Forward"
STATEHOOD: May 29, 1848
POSTAL ABBREVIATION: WI

WORDS TO KNOW

Moraine Lake

"Moraine" is a term that can mean anything left behind by a retreating glacier: boulders, trees, mounds of soil—and, yes, lakes. Moraine lakes are usually deep holes dug by an advancing glacier and then filled by the melt water left behind when it retreats.

Fun Facts

GET YOUR MOTOR RUNNING

Perhaps Wisconsin's most famous industrial product is the Harley-Davidson motorcycle. The Harley-Davidson company was founded in Racine, Wisconsin, in 1903. That year it produced three motorcycles. Since then, it has produced hundreds of thousands of motorcycles!

the local tribes. The one exception to this was the Fox tribe, who fought a fifty-year-long war with the French.

The French lost Wisconsin along with the rest of their North American possessions to the British in 1763. Twenty years later, the British gave up Wisconsin as part of the settlement of the American Revolution. Wisconsin was originally part of the Old Northwest Territory (which included all of what is now Ohio, Indiana, Illinois, Michigan, and Wisconsin, and part of Minnesota). Later, it became part of first the Illinois, then the Michigan Territory in 1818.

By the 1820s Wisconsin's lead mines had been opened up and were producing, and timber was being sold from land cleared for farming. By 1832, the remaining Native American tribes (mostly the Sauk and Fox) had had enough. They rebelled, were ruthlessly defeated in the short Black Hawk War, and removed to land west of the Mississippi River.

Wisconsin became a territory in 1836, and a state in 1848. Shortly before it became a state, Wisconsin lost claims to land surrounding Chicago, in northern Illinois, and also to what became Michigan's Upper Peninsula.

During the 1850s Wisconsin political leaders helped found the Republican Party, because Wisconsin was a firm anti-slavery state and the Republican Party was intended to be an abolitionist political party first and foremost. During the Civil War, many Wisconsinites served in the Union Army.

Wisconsin's radical streak stayed alive during the post–Civil War industrial boom. Politicians in Wisconsin founded the Progressive Party, and although the Party was eventually swallowed up by the Republican and Democratic parties, for a while the Progressives did elect some prominent leaders.

MINNESOTA: Land of 10,000 Lakes

Geography and Industry

Obviously, Minnesota, like its neighbor Wisconsin, has a lot of lakes. Most of these lakes were formed by a retreating ice sheet during the last ice age. Minnesota is also the state where the Mississippi River, the largest and most important river in America, gets its start. From its source at Lake Itasca in Minnesota, the mighty Mississippi runs over 2,300 miles to its mouth on the Gulf of Mexico, in Louisiana!

Rivers are as large a part of Minnesota's geography as are the state's many lakes. There are three major river systems in Minnesota. There is the Mississippi, which flows south; there is the Red River system, which flows north into Canada; and the eastern part of the state is drained by streams that flow eastward into Lake Superior.

Geographically speaking, Minnesota is a very diverse state. It has huge forests in the northern part of the state, several iron-rich mountain ranges in the eastern part of the state (the Mesabi, Cuyuna, and Vermillion ranges), and prairies in the central and southern parts of the state that make for very rich farmland.

Places like Voyageurs National Park and the Grand Portage and Pipestone National Monuments draw thousands of visitors per year. Minnesota is also a fishing paradise, with all of its lakes and streams and its access to Lake Superior.

History

Minnesota was dominated by the Ojibwa in the east and the Sioux on the western prairies when the French arrived to trade for furs in the mid-seventeenth century. The northeastern part of the state was ceded first to the British and then to the United States in the 1760s and the 1780s, respectively. The majority of the state was acquired by the United States in the Louisiana Purchase of 1803. The northern part came to the United States

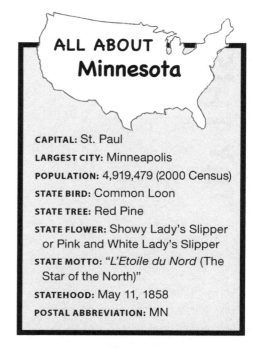

ALL ABOUT
Minnesota

CAPITAL: St. Paul

LARGEST CITY: Minneapolis

POPULATION: 4,919,479 (2000 Census)

STATE BIRD: Common Loon

STATE TREE: Red Pine

STATE FLOWER: Showy Lady's Slipper or Pink and White Lady's Slipper

STATE MOTTO: "*L'Etoile du Nord* (The Star of the North)"

STATEHOOD: May 11, 1858

POSTAL ABBREVIATION: MN

Fun Facts

MINNESOTA: NOT THE LAND OF 10,000 LAKES!

It's true! Minnesota's nickname is a mis-name. There are actually more than 10,000 lakes in Minnesota. In fact, there are over 12,000 in the state. This means that whoever came up with Minnesota's nickname got it wrong by over 2,000 lakes!

TRY THIS!

Visit the Spam Museum!

Did you know that there is a museum devoted to the canned meat known as Spam? It's true! It's in Minnesota (home of Hormel, the company that makes Spam), and it's called The Spam Museum. It's located at 1937 SPAM Boulevard, in Austin, Minnesota (1937 is the year that Hormel introduced Spam to the public).

in an 1818 treaty establishing part of the border between the United States and Canada.

Minnesota became a territory in 1849. The Panic (economic depression) of 1857 hit the territory very hard, because so many people had invested in various land schemes that wound up losing them money. Statehood came in 1858, and the Civil War in 1861.

While most of the army was away fighting in the southern states, the Minnesota Sioux went to war in 1862 against the U.S. government. It was a bloody uprising. Nearly 300 people on both sides were killed before the Sioux were suppressed.

Another momentous event that occurred in 1862 had a large impact on Minnesota. That year, Congress passed the Homestead Act, which gave "160 acres and a mule" to every settler who could stake out and farm a given tract of land for five years. Settlers flocked to Minnesota as a result.

During the post–Civil War period, large iron deposits were found in Minnesota's eastern mountains. For decades afterward, miners worked these deposits, until they were all but depleted. To this day, the largest open pit iron mine in the world is in Minnesota.

Several of America's most established food brands began in Minnesota. These include Pillsbury and Hormel.

Stretching unbroken from the Canadian border in the north down to the Oklahoma country in the south, the Great Plains both divide and bind together the North American continent. This part of the country is now known as America's Breadbasket because it grows enough grain collectively to feed the people of the world several times over. Wheat, oats, barley, and corn are grown all over the Great Plains.

And yet most people once called this region the Great American Desert! Before the steel plow was invented, there wasn't any blade strong enough to cut through the prairie sod of the plains, and so Americans viewed the Great Plains as an obstacle to be crossed on their way to places on the West Coast, like California.

The plains states are places of wide skies and broad horizons, of sudden tornadoes and baking hot, cloudless days. They are bordered by huge mountains in the west, and the broad Mississippi in the east. And they are crossed from northwest to southeast by a number of vast river systems of their own.

NORTH DAKOTA: The Peace Garden State

Geography and Industry

North Dakota is equal parts desolate (the western part of the state) and fertile (the eastern part of the state). The Missouri and Red rivers both flow through the state, and farming (wheat, flax, and corn) is good along their valleys. But the western part of the state is high desert, where very little grows. This region was so hard to travel through that early explorers nicknamed it the "badlands." The name stuck.

Nowadays people don't try to avoid the badlands. They go out of their way to see these rugged rock formations. Tourism has become an important industry in North Dakota.

North Dakota is almost entirely an agricultural state, and it is one of the most rural states left in the nation. There

ALL ABOUT North Dakota

CAPITAL: Bismarck

LARGEST CITY: Fargo

POPULATION: 642,200 (2000 Census)

STATE BIRD: Western Meadowlark

STATE TREE: American Elm

STATE FLOWER: Wild Prairie Rose

STATE MOTTO: "Liberty and Union, Now and Forever, One and Inseparable"

STATEHOOD: November 2, 1889

POSTAL ABBREVIATION: ND

is little industry to speak of besides mining, farming, and ranching in North Dakota. Oil was discovered in the 1950s, and is North Dakota's leading mineral export. Not long after, natural gas fields were uncovered as well. There are also salt, sand, gravel, and lime mining operations in the state.

Weather-wise, North Dakota is a tough place to live. The climate is harsh: hot, humid summers, sometimes plagued by tornadoes or drought, and frigid winters, consistently among the coldest in the continental United States. Because of its location in the far northern part of the country, directly south of Canada's great plains, there is nothing to keep polar weather from sweeping down along the Canadian Shield and directly into North Dakota.

History

Before European fur traders visited the region, semi-nomadic tribes such as the Arikara (Ree), Hidatsa (Gros Ventres), and Mandan farmed North Dakota's fertile river valleys for part of the year, then hunted buffalo during the other part. When the horse was introduced to the northern plains starting in the sixteenth and seventeenth centuries, tribes such as the Sioux, Cheyenne, Ojibwa, Cree, and Assiniboin abandoned farming, and moved out on the plains to follow the great buffalo herds year-round.

The Lewis and Clark Expedition spent the winter of 1804–05 with the Mandan tribe before making their way to the Pacific coast. Within twenty years, the Mandans had been literally wiped out by European diseases such as smallpox, cholera, whooping cough, mumps, and measles.

We know these diseases as childhood diseases, and today, hardly anyone dies from them. But the Native Americans did not have any immunity to these diseases, and so died by the thousands from them. This had happened to other tribes

Fun Facts

WHO ARE THE DAKOTAS NAMED AFTER?

North and South Dakota take their names from a band of the Sioux called the Dakota. There are other bands, with names like Lakota, etc., but the two states are named after the ones whose name starts with the "D"!

WORDS TO KNOW

Rural

A rural area is the opposite of an urban area, which means that a rural area is a relatively unpopulated place—still wild, with no cities and few roads or houses. Cultivated farmland is also considered a rural area, since it guarantees that there is no room for a city.

Fun Facts

ROOSEVELT THE COWBOY

In the 1880s future U.S. President Theodore Roosevelt established a working cattle ranch in the badlands of western North Dakota. Roosevelt spent three years working as a cowboy on his own ranch. He identified himself as a cowboy at heart for the rest of his life!

farther east as Europeans explored and settled North America, but out on the plains it seemed to happen even faster.

In 1818 the United States acquired part of the Red River Valley from British Canada, in exchange for some land drained by the Missouri River farther north. This land became part of the Dakota Territory when it was organized in 1851. The territory included land that eventually became the states of North and South Dakota, Wyoming, and Montana. Also in 1851, the first permanent American settlement was established in North Dakota, at a place called Pembina.

During the next few decades, the Native Americans living on the plains fought a series of wars with the U.S. Army, trying to stop the tide of white settlement. The Sioux and the Cheyenne fought especially hard. North Dakota was finally being settled because the new transcontinental railroad made travel and shipping of goods through and across the area much easier.

Things got really bad in the 1870s, with Sioux and Cheyenne warriors raiding all across the northern plains. By 1877, Native American resistance had ended.

The very next year, the first cattle ranch was established in North Dakota. Among those easterners who eventually came west to try their luck raising cattle was a young New Yorker named Theodore Roosevelt.

North Dakota became a state in late 1889, just minutes ahead of South Dakota, its neighbor to (not surprisingly) the south. Both states list the same day (November 2, 1889) as the day they became states.

Rock 'n' Roll

Break the letter codes to get the silly riddle and its silly answer!

HINT: **You will need to write the alphabet on a piece of paper, and write the numbers from 1 to 26 underneath. A=1, B=2, C=3, etc.!**

23rd	F+2	1st	R+2	♭		19th	before P	21st	S+1	J-2
A+3	E-4	L-1	after N	V-2	Z-25	14th				
18th	M+2	3rd	J+1		F+1	S-1	Q-2	T+1	16th	
8th	1st	19th		D+2	M+2	21st	P+2			
L+1	5th	14th		Z-3	8th	Q-2				
4th	M+2	P-2	20th			19th	G+2	14th	I-2	?
after L	Q-2	V-1	M+1	20th						
Q+1	21st	before T	8th	before N	N+1	after Q	5th			!

SOUTH DAKOTA: The Mount Rushmore State

Geography and Industry

South Dakota has three separate geographic regions within its borders: the prairies in the east, the Great Plains in the middle, and the Black Hills in the west. The Black Hills are a small range of mountains that rise up to a height of 7,000 feet at their highest point, right in the middle of the plains. They have been sacred to the surrounding tribes of Native Americans for centuries. Because the Black Hills are covered with forests, an early explorer described them as "an island of trees in a sea of grass."

★ ★ ★ ★ ★ ★ ★ 67 ★ ★ ★ ★ ★ ★ ★

ALL ABOUT South Dakota

CAPITAL: Pierre

LARGEST CITY: Sioux City

POPULATION: 754,844 (2000 Census)

STATE BIRD: Ring-Necked Pheasant

STATE TREE: Black Hills Spruce

STATE FLOWER: Pasqueflower

STATE MOTTO: "Under God the People Rule"

STATEHOOD: November 2, 1889

POSTAL ABBREVIATION: SD

TRY THIS!

Hot Springs

Evans' Plunge, in Hot Springs, South Dakota, is fed by a natural hot spring. Hot springs are usually a result of volcanic activity in the region. Are there any hot springs near where you live? Go to your library or use the Internet to find out.

The Missouri River Valley is very wide where it runs south through the central part of South Dakota. Other important rivers in the state include the Cheyenne, the Big Sioux, the James, and the White. The climate in South Dakota is pretty much the same as that of North Dakota, with frigid winters and hot, humid summers.

Tourism is very important to South Dakota's economy, and the massive patriotic sculpture of Mount Rushmore is visited by millions of tourists every year, as are such attractions as Badlands National Park and Wind Cave National Park. There is also some hot spring activity in the region, and there are spas at places like the appropriately named Hot Springs.

Farming is also important, and South Dakota is a major producer of grains (wheat, barley, oats, etc.), corn, sunflowers, flax, sorghum, and soybeans. Where oil is North Dakota's major mineral product, gold is South Dakota's.

The Sioux and the Black Hills

When the first French fur traders visited the region during the eighteenth century, two large tribes of Native Americans lived in what is now South Dakota. The Sioux were horse-breeding, buffalo-hunting nomads, and the Arikara lived and farmed the wide river bottoms in the valleys of the Missouri and South Dakota's other large rivers. The Sioux considered the Black Hills sacred (their descendants still do), in much the same way that Jews, Christians, and Muslims today have considered the lands of Israel and Palestine sacred for centuries.

By the 1840s the Sioux were in sole possession of South Dakota, having chased the Arikara north into North Dakota and Canada. They did not enjoy sole ownership of the region for long. As happened in North Dakota, the transcontinental railroads began to open up South Dakota to settlement beginning in the 1850s.

The Homestead Act of 1862 made settlement of South Dakota even more appealing to thousands of farm families

looking for "free" land. The Sioux didn't like this, and went on the warpath several times during the 1860s. Finally, the Sioux and the U.S. government signed a treaty in 1868 giving the Sioux a reservation in their sacred Black Hills. It seemed as if there might be peace in South Dakota after years of tension between the Native Americans and white settlers.

These good feelings lasted less than six years. In 1874, gold was discovered in the Black Hills, and gold fever struck South Dakota. Try as it might, the U.S. Army could not keep gold-hungry prospectors out of the Sioux's reservation. War soon followed.

At first, the Sioux and their allies won some brilliant victories against the army. They defeated a cavalry detachment under General Nelson Miles at the Battle of the Rosebud, and lured Colonel George Armstrong Custer and his Seventh Cavalry to their doom at the Little Big Horn in 1876. Sioux leaders such as Sitting Bull and Crazy Horse rallied their warriors time and again to fight for their sacred Black Hills.

But eventually, as had happened so many times before, the whites had better weapons and more soldiers. By 1877, the last of the Sioux wars was over. The United States "bought" the Black Hills from the defeated Native Americans (no money was ever paid out). Just over a decade afterward, South Dakota became the fortieth state.

As late as 1980, the U.S. government offered the Sioux $100,000,000 as compensation for taking the Black Hills from them. The Sioux have refused all such offers. They say they want the Black Hills back.

IOWA: The Hawkeye State

Geography and Industry

The terrain of Iowa is a combination of rolling hills and broad prairies. The Mississippi River borders Iowa on the east, and

ALL ABOUT Iowa

CAPITAL: Des Moines

LARGEST CITY: Des Moines

POPULATION: 2,926,324 (2000 Census)

STATE BIRD: Eastern Goldfinch

STATE TREE: Oak

STATE FLOWER: Wild Rose

STATE MOTTO: "Our Liberties We Prize and Our Rights We Will Maintain"

STATEHOOD: December 28, 1846

POSTAL ABBREVIATION: IA

Fun Facts

THE WORLD'S SHORTEST AND STEEPEST RAILROAD

Did you know that there is a railroad that has a 60-degree grade (that is *steep*!) and is less than 300 feet long? It's true! The world's shortest railroad is in Dubuque, Iowa, and measures only 296 feet!

two-thirds of Iowa's rivers and streams flow eastward into the Mississippi. The Missouri River flows along Iowa's western border. Iowa was once covered by hardwood forests, but logging and clearing of the area for farming destroyed much of them. Farm fields also took their toll on Iowa's original prairies in much the same way.

Iowa has some of the richest farmland in the world. Almost three-quarters of the state's land is still farmland! In Iowa, farmland means a bit of hay, a bit of oats, and some soybeans, but most of all it means corn. And that corn in turn often goes to feed prize-winning Iowa hogs (which means that these hogs are "corn-fed," naturally!).

Aside from farming, Iowa also supports such farming-dependent industries as food processing (which makes sense, because so much food is produced in Iowa). Another important industry is the manufacture of farm machinery (which also makes sense!).

Outdoor recreation including hunting and fishing are pivotal to Iowa. Iowa is in the path of migratory birds like ducks and geese. These birds and the European pheasant, among others, are hunted in the autumn. With so many rivers running in and around Iowa, there is year-round fishing there as well.

History

Long before the coming of the Europeans to what is now Iowa, the Mississippian culture flourished here. These people were mound builders, like their neighbors throughout the Mississippi and Ohio River valleys. Their culture collapsed and they disappeared around 1500.

When the first French explorers visited the region, there were a number of Native American tribes living there. These included the Sauk and Fox, the Sioux, and the Iowa (a tribe from which the state gets its name).

After the United States acquired Iowa as part of the Louisiana Purchase in 1803, settlers began moving across the Mississippi River and cutting down Iowa's forest and plowing under its prairies, converting the state to agriculture. After the disastrous Black Hawk War (1832) the remaining Native Americans were removed across the Missouri River to Indian Territory (what is now Oklahoma). Within a decade Iowa had not just river access to eastern markets for its corn and other vegetables, but railroad access as well.

NEBRASKA: The Cornhusker State

Geography and Industry

The Missouri River forms part of Nebraska's northeastern border. The other major river system that passes through Nebraska is the Platte. The Platte is formed in western Nebraska where the North Platte and South Platte rivers meet. The Platte itself flows into the Missouri near Nebraska's largest city, Omaha. Eastern Nebraska is very fertile soil, and it's mostly farmland, especially along the river bottoms. The majority of Nebraska's population lives in eastern Nebraska. Eastern Nebraska's farmers grow mostly grains such as wheat and barley, or hay and alfalfa for feeding hogs and cattle and other animals.

Cities such as Lincoln and Omaha are the hubs of the insurance industry, which is centered in eastern Nebraska.

Western Nebraska is cattle country. Nebraska is currently the second leading cattle-producing state in the United States! Western Nebraska has lots of sand dunes and sandstone rock formations. These formations shelter small valleys of grass that are ideal ranges for cattle grazing.

One of these formations is Scott's Bluff, which is very close to Nebraska's western border with Wyoming. It's at the center of the Scott's Bluff National Monument, which is part of the Oregon

ALL ABOUT Nebraska

CAPITAL: Lincoln
LARGEST CITY: Omaha
POPULATION: 1,711,263
STATE BIRD: Western Meadowlark
STATE TREE: Cottonwood
STATE FLOWER: Goldenrod
STATE MOTTO: "Equality Before the Law"
STATEHOOD: March 1, 1867
POSTAL ABBREVIATION: NE

Trail, and is quite a tourist spot. Other places in Nebraska that are popular with tourists include the Fort Niobara Wildlife Refuge and Father Flanagan's Boys Town in Omaha.

History

Mound-building Native Americans who were members of the Mississippian culture lived in eastern Nebraska up until the culture disappeared, around 1500. The first Europeans visited the region not long afterward when Spanish conquistadors under the command of Francisco Vasquez de Coronado entered Nebraska, looking for gold. They didn't find anything but native villages and rolling prairie.

Such Native American tribes as the Pawnee, Ponca, Osage, and Oto lived in what is now Nebraska when the French arrived to trade for furs in the eighteenth century. The Ponca, Osage, and Oto farmed in the fertile eastern river valleys. The Pawnee were nomads who hunted buffalo out in western Nebraska.

The French claimed Nebraska for themselves, and in 1803 they sold it to the United States as part of the Louisiana Purchase. Explorers such as the Lewis and Clark Expedition (1804–06) and Zebulon Pike's expedition (1806) helped map out much of the area for the United States. It was just a few years later (1813) that the first permanent settlement in Nebraska was established: a trading post at Bellevue.

Beginning in 1819, steamboats ran up and down the Missouri River. Omaha quickly boomed into a bustling river port. When settlers began moving west, along what eventually became known as the Oregon Trail, on their way to settle the Pacific Coast, Nebraskans made a lot of profit by selling them supplies.

In 1854 Nebraska became a territory as a result of the complicated Kansas-Nebraska Act, which allowed people in U.S. territories to vote and decide for themselves whether or

WORDS TO KNOW

Nomad

Nomads are groups of people who don't live in any single position, place, or situation for very long. Most of the buffalo-hunting plains tribes of North America were nomadic.

Unicameral

Nebraska is the only state in the Union to have a state government that is unicameral. This means that rather than having two houses, such as a house of representatives and a senate, as our national government does (a bicameral legislature), the state legislature of Nebraska has only one house. There is no state senate in Nebraska.

not their territories (and eventually their states) would be slave states (states where slavery was legal) or free states (states where slavery was outlawed). During the Civil War that followed soon after, Nebraska was a free territory, and entered the Union shortly after the end of the war, in 1867.

KANSAS: The Sunflower State

Geography and Industry

Kansas is wheat country. It is an even tableland that rises gradually from the lowland prairies in the eastern part of Kansas to the much drier western plains that border the foothills of the Rocky Mountains, in neighboring Colorado. The major rivers that drain the state are the Arkansas and the Kansas rivers, both of which flow southeastward through Kansas on their way to the Mississippi (although the Kansas River flows into the Missouri River first).

The climate is good for wheat, but can be hard on humans. Hot and humid in the eastern part and hot and dry in the western part during the summer months (which are also tornado season), Kansas can be bitterly cold during the winter (which is the blizzard season).

As stated above, Kansas is a wheat state. In fact, many people would say that Kansas is *the* wheat state! Kansas is the number-one-producing wheat state in the country. For a very long time, farming was Kansas's leading industry. In addition to wheat, the state also produces plenty of sorghum and corn, and beef cattle.

But farming is no longer Kansas's leading industry. Nowadays Kansas is a leading maker of computer parts and transportation equipment such as airplanes. Lots of planes are now built in Wichita, which has become an aerospace town.

ALL ABOUT Kansas

CAPITAL: Topeka
LARGEST CITY: Wichita
POPULATION: 2,688,418 (2000 Census)
STATE BIRD: Western Meadowlark
STATE TREE: Cottonwood
STATE FLOWER: Native Sunflower
STATE MOTTO: *"Ad Astra per Aspera* (To the Stars Through Adversity)"
STATEHOOD: January 29, 1861
POSTAL ABBREVIATION: KS

WORDS TO KNOW

Tornado

A tornado is a weather phenomenon that causes air to spin in ever-tighter circles until it forms what is known as a funnel cloud. This spinning storm can be like a top, sliding all over a vast area and crushing everything in its path. Tornadoes are usually very destructive and often fatal, so be careful if you ever see one in person!

History

The first Europeans to visit Kansas were the members of the Spanish conquistador Coronado's expedition, which passed through in 1541. They were searching for gold. They found a mostly flat, rolling country cut by huge, fast-flowing rivers.

When the French arrived to claim the region as their own and make it part of the sprawling Louisiana country in the late seventeenth century, there were several large tribes of Native Americans living in what is now Kansas. These tribes included the Kansa (for whom the state is named), the Osage, the Wichita, and the Pawnee.

When horses were introduced into the region, many of the Native Americans quit farming in the eastern part of the state, and moved out onto the plains to become nomadic buffalo hunters. The Pawnee in particular became skilled trackers and hunters on horseback. Many of them later worked for the U.S. Army as scouts in the government's wars against other tribes.

Because much of Kansas was covered in prairie grass that was too thick to be plowed, it was seen as part of the Great American Desert. Is it any wonder that many of those Native Americans you've been reading about in the previous chapters wound up getting sent to the "desert" part of Kansas? Many others were removed even farther south into what was then called Indian Territory, and what we today call Oklahoma.

Because it was close to Missouri and other southern border states, Kansas got caught up in the struggle over slavery during the decade preceding the American Civil War (1861–65). There was a bitter struggle between people who had moved to Kansas from slave states, such as Missouri, and wanted Kansas as another slave state for the Union, and those people who had come to settle Kansas from the northern free states.

This was a mini civil war that preceded the larger one that occurred across the country just a couple of years afterward. This fight and the territory itself were referred to as Bleeding Kansas.

You Live Where?

Figure out the word equations and picture puzzles to learn some silly but real names for cities in the Southern Plains!

The Southern Plains stretch from Missouri into Colorado, from the Gulf of Mexico to the Guadalupe Mountains in the west. They are broad and flat in places, rolling and hilly in others, and they rise into interesting rock formations and tablelands called mesas in others.

The Southern Plains experience serious extremes of temperature over the course of the year: cold in the winter and blazing hot in the summer. They are subject to some of the worst hailstorms and tornadoes in recorded history. These states have amazing mineral wealth, including oil, natural gas, and coal. They have rich farmland, and a couple of them (Louisiana and Texas) have huge and interesting populations.

The Southern Plains are also a rich mix of different cultures. Originally settled in places by the French and Spanish (and the Mexicans), and occupied continuously in others by a variety of Native American cultures, these states are a fascinating mosaic of the diversity the United States is capable of, even while the skyline seems unrelentingly the same throughout the region.

MISSOURI: The Show Me State
Geography and Industry

The Missouri River splits the state into three parts. The northern part is flat prairie that is like the land in Iowa. Also like Iowa, this part of Missouri is very rich farmland. Farmers grow lots of corn there, and raise livestock such as cattle and hogs. The Missouri River valley is also largely farmland, although

★ ★ ★ ★ ★ ★ ★ ★

the state's large cities—Kansas City in the west and St. Louis in the east—have attracted much heavy industry.

St. Louis lies at the juncture of the Missouri and Mississippi rivers. This location has led to both remarkable growth and quite a lot of history for the city that has long been considered the gateway to the west. This is in no small part because St. Louis sits at a crossroads of various parts of the nation. It is right at the center where north meets south, and both meet west. This makes it a bit of a cultural melting pot.

Directly south of the Missouri River lie the Ozark highlands, which include both mountains and foothills. The eastern part is more rugged, with the western part more rolling hill country.

The southwestern part of the state is part of the Great Plains, and rolls westward into Oklahoma. The main crops grown on these plains are livestock fodder, such as hay and alfalfa. Since cattle, sheep, and hogs are raised in this region as well, farmers don't have to go far to find customers for their crops!

Around Cape Girardeau in the southeast is the "bootheel" part of the state. This part of the state was swampland when Missouri was originally settled. Around the time that the United States acquired the territory as part of the Louisiana Purchase in 1803, a drainage system was devised that allowed the swampland to be converted into cotton plantations.

Missouri is not just an agricultural state, though. In cities like St. Louis, the aerospace industry is well represented. Airplane parts are made throughout the state also. In Kansas City, cars, trucks, other types of transportation equipment (buses, tractors, etc.), and vending machines are built.

History

Before European exploration and settlement of the area, there were a number of Native American tribes who lived in

ALL ABOUT Missouri

CAPITAL: Jefferson City

LARGEST CITY: Kansas City

POPULATION: 5,595,211 (2000 Census)

STATE BIRD: Bluebird

STATE TREE: Dogwood

STATE FLOWER: Hawthorn

STATE MOTTO: "*Salus Populi Suprema Lex Esto* (The Welfare of the People Shall Be the Supreme Law)"

STATEHOOD: August 10, 1821

POSTAL ABBREVIATION: MO

Fun Facts

MISSOURI'S "BOOTHEEL"

When Missouri was ready to become a state, it turned out that it was a few thousand people short of the number required to become a state. So Congress shaved off what we now call the "bootheel" from the Arkansas Territory, and added it to Missouri in order to make its population high enough to qualify it for statehood!

TRY THIS!

Places to See

If you're in St. Louis, make sure you check out the Peace Arch. It's an amazing piece of architecture. Other places to see in Missouri include Kansas City's Nelson-Atkins Museum of Art, the Museum of the American Indian in St. Joseph, and the Harry S Truman Memorial Library in Independence.

the region, including the Osage, the Oto, and of course, the Missouri, for whom the state is named. The French were the first Europeans to settle in the region, establishing a lead mine at Sainte Genevieve in 1735. To this day, lead mining is an important part of Missouri's economy.

From 1735 until 1763, the French controlled Missouri. In 1763, they ceded Missouri along with the rest of their North American lands to the Spanish. Under Napoleon, the French got Missouri (and the rest of French Louisiana) back from the Spanish, but with the condition that they never turn it over to the United States. Napoleon promptly broke that agreement, and sold the entire area to the United States for about $3,000,000. What a bargain that turned out to be!

Missouri entered the Union as a result of the Missouri Compromise (see the Maine section of Chapter 1 for an explanation of the Missouri Compromise) in 1820. Because many of the people from the United States who moved in to help settle Missouri were originally from the South, and because Missouri had some land near Cape Girardeau that was under cotton cultivation, Missouri came into the Union as a slave state.

Surprisingly enough, when the Civil War finally came between the North and the South, Missouri stayed in the Union, although citizens of the state fought on both sides of the conflict, as was the case in other border states (see Chapter 3, Kentucky).

ARKANSAS: The Natural State
Geography and Industry

Like Missouri to the north, Arkansas is both on the western bank of the Mississippi River and bisected by a large river flowing eastward through the state into the Mississippi. Also like Missouri, the river running through Arkansas bears the same name as the state (the Arkansas River).

Other important rivers in Arkansas include the White, the Ouachita (pronounced WA-shee-taw), and the Red. The Red River marks part of Arkansas' western border with Texas.

Arkansas is a very hilly state. In the north lie the Ozark Mountains, and to the southwest are the Ouachita Mountains. The Ozarks are so rugged that the people who settled there became highly isolated and very independent.

The lowlands along the Mississippi and Arkansas River systems are rich farmland where cotton is still a major crop. Since the Civil War, though, Arkansas has grown many other crops. These other crops include two that are now much more important than cotton: rice and soybeans. Catfish are actually raised on Arkansas fish farms for sale to restaurants and grocery stores. Broiler chickens, turkeys, and dairy products also play a significant role in the state's economy.

Arkansas has many other products aside from agricultural products. These include things like natural gas, petroleum (oil), lumber, furniture, chemicals, aircraft parts, automobile parts, and other types of machinery.

Although hiking and camping are important recreational activities in Arkansas, they are not as popular as hunting and fishing are. This includes fishing for (you guessed it) catfish!

History

Before European exploration and settlement, Native Americans lived in Arkansas dating back to at least 500 A.D., when Native Americans called the Bluff Dwellers settled into caves along the Arkansas River. They were followed by Mound Builders of the Mississippian civilization, who built their trademark mounds in the major river valleys of the region. By the time of first contact with Europeans, such tribes as the Oto and the Osage were living in the region, splitting their time between farming and hunting/gathering.

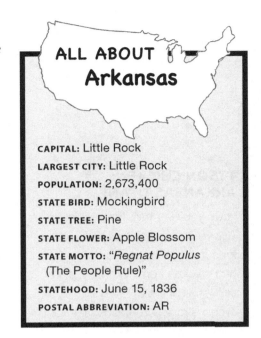

ALL ABOUT Arkansas

CAPITAL: Little Rock
LARGEST CITY: Little Rock
POPULATION: 2,673,400
STATE BIRD: Mockingbird
STATE TREE: Pine
STATE FLOWER: Apple Blossom
STATE MOTTO: "*Regnat Populus* (The People Rule)"
STATEHOOD: June 15, 1836
POSTAL ABBREVIATION: AR

WORDS TO KNOW

Bisect

The word "bisect" means to split or cut in two.

Fun Facts

TYSON CHICKEN: ARKANSAS TITAN!

Have you ever had Tyson chicken? Ask your parents if you don't know for sure. If you have, you likely had chicken from Arkansas, since almost all of the chicken sold by Tyson is raised in Arkansas. In fact, over *one billion* chickens are raised in Arkansas for sale for the dinner table each year alone!

ALL ABOUT Louisiana

CAPITAL: Baton Rouge

LARGEST CITY: New Orleans

POPULATION: 4,468,976 (2000 Census)

STATE BIRD: Eastern Brown Pelican

STATE TREE: Cypress

STATE FLOWER: Magnolia

STATE MOTTO: "Union, Justice, and Confidence"

STATEHOOD: April 30, 1812

POSTAL ABBREVIATION: LA

Spanish explorer Hernando de Soto and his expedition visited Arkansas in the early 1540s. De Soto and his men crossed and recrossed the state, headed first away from the Mississippi and into Oklahoma, then back to the Mississippi, all while looking for gold and silver.

The French eventually settled Arkansas during the seventeenth century, although during the French colonial period there were never as many people living in Arkansas as were living in New Orleans to the south, or around St. Louis to the north. Along with the rest of French Louisiana (the area of North America under French control west of the Mississippi River), Arkansas changed hands a number of times in the eighteenth century, before being sold to the United States as part of the Louisiana Purchase in 1803.

Having entered the Union in 1836 as a slave state, Arkansas seceded with ten other southern states in 1861. Battles such as Pea Ridge were fought in the northern part of the state, but the most important Civil War action that occurred in Arkansas was the naval battle between Union and Confederate forces for control of the Mississippi River.

LOUISIANA: The Pelican State

Geography and Industry

While it's true that there are swamps in Louisiana, and bayous, and cays, and crocodiles, there is a lot more to the Cajun state than hurricanes, hoodoos, and humidity.

For example, Louisiana is a leading agricultural producer. They grow an amazing amount of food: corn, pecans, soybeans, hay, sweet potatoes, sugarcane, rice, cotton, and strawberries. Also, fishing is a very important industry in Louisiana. Oysters, shrimp, and crayfish are all plentiful in Louisiana's waters, and figure prominently in local (Cajun) cuisine.

Like its neighbors Texas and Oklahoma, Louisiana has large deposits of crude oil (petroleum) and natural gas. Most of Louisiana's oil deposits are offshore, and the state has a thriving oil industry that includes large refineries that turn crude oil into motor oil and gas. These refineries and the rest of the oil industry employ large parts of Louisiana's population.

Timber (mostly pine forests) covers over half of the state. As a result, lumber and paper are also very important exports from Louisiana.

Louisiana has hundreds of small offshore islands, and the mighty Mississippi completes its 2,000-plus-mile journey across the continent and flows into the Gulf of Mexico in southern Louisiana. The coastal region is very rainy, fitting the stereotype of a swampy Louisiana made up of little other than marshes. There are large lagoons made up of standing fresh water. The largest of these is Lake Pontchartrain, which is the lake on the banks of which the city of New Orleans was built.

Speaking of New Orleans, it is one of the most colorful and distinctive cities in America. The birthplace of jazz and blues music, and home to Cajun cuisine, New Orleans is a very popular tourist attraction, especially during the early spring, which is Mardi Gras season. "Mardi Gras" is French for "Fat Tuesday," and it takes place in the famous French Quarter of the city. It is a tradition that has been ongoing in New Orleans since 1838!

Central, western, and northern Louisiana are a little like the French bayou country. Central Louisiana is full of pine forests and prairies, and northern Louisiana is very hilly. Baton Rouge, the state capital, is located in central Louisiana.

History

Louisiana was originally the home of such Native American tribes as the Choctaw, Natchez, and Caddo. The Spanish were the first Europeans to visit the region, but established

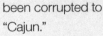

WORDS TO KNOW

Bayou

A bayou is a small slow-moving stream or creek usually found in low-lying areas.

Cajun

When France lost its Canadian colony of Acadia to the English, the English forced many of the Acadian settlers to leave. Thousands of these settlers moved to the other major French holding in North America: the Louisiana bayou country around New Orleans. Since they moved there nearly 300 years ago, the name "Acadian" has been corrupted to "Cajun."

Fun Facts

CRAYFISH

Crayfish are freshwater lobsters. They are smaller than their ocean-going cousins, and are highly prized by Cajun cooks. Nearly 100 percent of all crayfish caught and eaten in the United States are caught in Louisiana!

no lasting presence. In 1682 Robert de La Salle came south down the Mississippi to its mouth in what is now Louisiana, and claimed all of the lands drained by the river for France. The lands on the western side of the Mississippi were named Louisiana in honor of La Salle's king, Louis XIV of France.

New Orleans was founded in 1718. It quickly became the largest and most important city in French Louisiana. After the English took the French Canadian province of Acadia, thousands of French-speaking Acadians moved down the Mississippi and settled in French Louisiana. Today, there are as many as 500,000 of their descendants living in southern Mississippi, southern Louisiana, and eastern Texas.

After the United States acquired all of Louisiana in 1803, settlers poured into the area from the neighboring southern states and territories. The Louisiana territory entered the Union as the state of Louisiana in 1812, the same year that the United States fought its second war with England.

At the time that the Civil War broke out, there were more slaves than free people living in the state. Louisiana seceded in 1861. Because of its location next to the mouth of the Mississippi, Louisiana saw much fighting, especially along the Mississippi River. New Orleans was captured by Union forces in early 1862, and the entire river was under Union control by July 1863, when the last Confederate fortress on the river (Vicksburg) surrendered.

Life in LA

Louisiana has been the hangout for two different kinds of critters that both start with the letter P. One critter is historical, and the other is still there today! First, connect the dots. Then, break the "First to Last" and the "Vowel Switch" codes to learn about these Louisiana residents.

heT

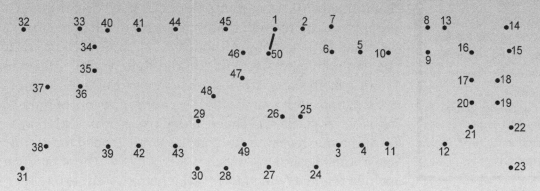

eanJ afitteL adh a ideawayh ni ouisianaL.

Tha briwn

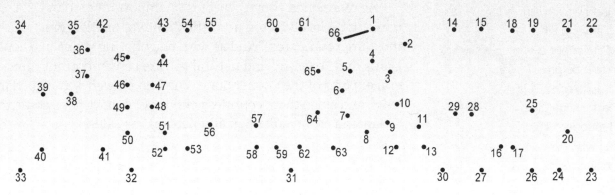

es tha Lioeseunu stuta berd.

ALL ABOUT Oklahoma

CAPITAL: Oklahoma City

LARGEST CITY: Oklahoma City

POPULATION: 3,450,654 (2000 Census)

STATE BIRD: Scissor-Tailed Flycatcher

STATE TREE: Redbud

STATE FLOWER: Mistletoe

STATE MOTTO: "*Labor Omnia Vincit* (Labor Conquers All Things)"

STATEHOOD: November 16, 1907

POSTAL ABBREVIATION: OK

WORDS TO KNOW

Sooner!

In 1890, the last great land rush of the nineteenth century took place in what is now western Oklahoma. Free land was available for the taking to anyone who could stake out a claim to it before anyone else did. This is where we get the word "sooner." The people who got their claims filed fastest were there sooner than anyone else!

OKLAHOMA: The Sooner State

Geography and Industry

Have you ever heard the song lyric from the musical Oklahoma that goes: "O-kla-HOMA where the wind goes whippin' down the plain"? (Ask your parents, or maybe your grandparents, about it.) Well, that lyric pretty much sums up Oklahoma's geography. Although it has some high mesas in the panhandle (western) part of the state, and the Ouachita Mountains in the southwest, the state is overwhelmingly open plains, with lots of wheat farming, and lots of grazing land for cattle and sheep. Large rivers cross Oklahoma from the northwest to the southeast, all headed for drainage in the Mississippi, which is farther east. These big rivers include the Red (which forms Oklahoma's southern border with neighboring Texas), the Canadian, and the Cimarron.

The weather on Oklahoma's plains can get pretty extreme. In the winter it gets very cold, because the wind whips from farther north, and there is nothing (hills, mountains, etc.) to stop it. In the summers the sun bakes the plains pretty thoroughly.

As mentioned above, wheat is an important crop in Oklahoma (it replaced cotton after the Civil War as Oklahoma's most important crop). And as with neighboring states like Louisiana and Texas, oil and natural gas are *very* important mineral exports of the Sooner State. The first oil well was drilled in 1888, and since then, countless billions of dollars have come to Oklahoma as a result of oil and natural gas sales!

History

Before European exploration and settlement, tribes like the Oto, the Osage, the Kansa, the Arapaho, and the Kiowa all lived in what is now Oklahoma. Interestingly enough, there was a time after the United States acquired Oklahoma when more Native Americans settled in eastern Oklahoma. This was because the United States designated parts of the Louisiana Purchase at various times as Indian territory.

TEXAS: The Lone Star State

Geography and Industry

Often when we think of Texas, we think of the desert and the plains. But Texas (like many other states) is surrounded by water. The Gulf of Mexico and the Rio Grande River border the Lone Star State on the southern side, the Sabine makes up a lot of its eastern border with Louisiana, and most of its northern border with Oklahoma is made up by the Red River.

Texas is huge! Not only is it the largest state in the continental United States (only Alaska is larger), it is the second-largest state population-wise (behind California).

In the east, Texas has hills covered in pine forests that spread between the Trinity River and the Sabine River where it borders Louisiana. These pine trees have led to the region developing quite a logging industry. There used to be huge cotton plantations here before the Civil War, but now rice is king. Most of the rice produced in Texas is produced in East Texas. There is also a lot of heavy industry in this region, with the cities of Port Arthur and Beaumont having much manufacturing within their city limits.

The north-central part of the state is prairie that has some of the richest soil in the country. And Dallas, which is in this region, has one of the fastest-growing industrial areas. Oil companies, agricultural conglomerates, and electronics and computer companies all have combined to help make Dallas an industrial force in the twenty-first century.

The high plains region in northern Texas has a lot of grazing land for cattle, even though it can get very cold there during the winters. (Texas is the number-one producer of beef in the

ALL ABOUT Texas

CAPITAL: Austin
LARGEST CITY: Houston
POPULATION: 20,851,820 (2000 Census)
STATE BIRD: Mockingbird
STATE TREE: Pecan
STATE FLOWER: Bluebonnet
STATE MOTTO: "Friendship"
STATEHOOD: December 29, 1845
POSTAL ABBREVIATION: TX

country.) West Texas is very arid and has a lot of rocky hills, rising as it does toward the neighboring Rocky Mountains. The Rio Grande border with Mexico is thousands of miles long.

Tourism is becoming a large industry in Texas. Padre Island National Seashore is a popular vacation spot, and the Johnson Space Center in Houston sees thousands of visitors annually. Outdoor recreation areas like Lake Meredith and Amistad National Recreation Areas and Guadalupe Mountains National Park offer breathtaking scenery for camping, fishing, hiking, and hunting.

History

Ancestors of the Caddo lived in Texas for thousands of years before the first Europeans visited. The Caddo lived mostly in the northwest, along the Red River, and were farmers who stayed put, rather than plains-dwellers. The Texas plains were home to tribes such as the Comanche, the Kiowa, and the Apache.

Spanish refugees from the Pueblo Revolt in New Mexico were the first Europeans to settle in Texas (see Chapter 9, New Mexico for more on the Pueblo Revolt). The French tried to settle along the Gulf Coast just three years later, moving westward from their base in Louisiana. This galvanized the Spanish settlers into strengthening their own claims to the region.

Around 1803, many Americans in the southern states were looking to Texas as prime cotton-growing country. Presidents such as James Monroe and John Quincy Adams tried to buy the region from Spain, but the Spanish were not interested.

After Mexico gained control of the land in the Mexican War of Independence, they did not want to part with Texas either, but they allowed Americans to emigrate there as settlers, as long as the Americans swore allegiance to the Mexican government. This rule worked only too well, because by 1830 there were three times as many American-born settlers in Texas as there were Mexicans. The Mexican government tried to crack down on the Americans in Texas and limit their trade with the

WORDS TO KNOW

Tejas!

Texas gets its name from the name of the first Spanish mission that was founded in the Lone Star State. The mission was established by Franciscan priests near the Neches River in 1690, and was called Mission San Francisco de los Tejas. "Tejas" meant "friends" and was referring to the local Native American population.

United States, but these attempts backfired, and pushed the Americans in Texas to think of independence from Mexico.

In late 1835 war broke out, and the Mexican dictator Antonio Lopez de Santa Anna invaded Texas at the head of a large Mexican army. He swore that he would crush the growing Texan rebellion. After wiping out the defenders of the Alamo and massacring several hundred Texan soldiers who had surrendered at Goliad, Santa Anna was caught completely by surprise by General Sam Houston's much smaller Texan army at the climactic battle of San Jacinto in 1836. Wounded and captured himself, Santa Anna granted Texas independence the next day, in exchange for his freedom. He later repudiated the treaty he signed, saying he did it because he was given no choice.

Texas Becomes a State

Texas was an independent republic for nearly a decade after it won independence from Mexico. Texans overwhelmingly wanted to be part of the United States, but there were obstacles to statehood. American politicians who feared worse relations with Mexico (which still claimed Texas) and wanted to halt the spread of American plantation slavery repeatedly blocked Congress's attempts to incorporate Texas.

By 1844 Texas's government was broke and in need of a bail-out. The English and French both offered to help, and that made the United States so nervous about having Texas in debt to European nations that President John Tyler was able to convince Congress to finally offer to annex Texas that year.

When the Civil War came, Texas seceded with the other states. Because of its vast open ranges and large supplies of cattle and grain, it was soon considered one of the "breadbaskets of the Confederacy." Once the Union Navy took control of the Mississippi River, though, Texas (along with Arkansas and Louisiana) was cut off completely from the rest of the South.

Totally Texas

Use the directions to figure out which words to cross out of the puzzle grid. When you are finished, read the remaining words from left to right and top to bottom. You will learn the silly answer to the math mystery!

Cross out...

...the three words of the Texas nickname.

...words that rhyme with DOOR.

...six-letter words that end in Y.

...numbers without the letter O.

"Talbott took twenty turtles to Texas to taste tacos."

How many letters T are in that?

twelve	there	lone
are	simply	four
more	thirteen	only
two	star	thirty
plenty	letters	ten
T	store	in
twenty	that	state

I magine a region with a skyline of jagged peaks that reach higher skyward than anywhere else in the continental United States. This is a place of broad plains and wide, rapid-running rivers, where everything is giant-sized. This is the Intermountain West, and the mountains are the Rockies.

Nothing is small in the Intermountain West. These mountains make mountains elsewhere in the country (like the eastern seaboard) seem more like hills. All of the large rivers that flow eastward across the Great Plains and into the Mississippi originate in the Intermountain West. Rivers such as the Missouri, the Arkansas, the Red, the Canadian, the Platte, and the Rio Grande all begin in the Rocky Mountains. So do the two great rivers of the west—the Colorado in the southwest and the Columbia (which rises in the Canadian Rockies) in the northwest.

MONTANA: The Treasure State

Geography

Montana takes its name from the Spanish word for "mountain country," but it is much more than a mountain state. Nearly two-thirds of Montana is on the western part of the Great Plains, and some parts of it are as flat as a table! These plains are one reason Montana is often called the Big Sky state, because on the Montana plains, the horizon is so low that most of what you see there is sky. Montana has mighty rivers running through it, such as the Missouri, the Milk, the Sun, and the Yellowstone (all of which actually drain into the Missouri).

However, Montana is "mountain country" for a reason. The Rocky Mountains run right through the western part of the state, and they include such famous ranges of mountains as the Cabinet Mountains and the rugged Bitterroot Range. The Continental Divide runs along the ridge of the Rockies, from northwestern Montana to the south central part of the state.

Montana is still mostly unpopulated. There are fewer than a million people in the state, which is not very many when you consider that Montana is the fourth largest state in America (only Alaska, Texas, and California are larger)! Montana's main industry these days is tourism, which has replaced mining and ranching.

There are so many places to see in Montana! There is Glacier-Waterton International Peace Park, Yellowstone National Park, and the Little Bighorn National Monument, which was the site of Custer's Last Stand. There are also plenty of places to hunt and fish, boat, hike, and camp, especially near Flathead Lake, a huge body of water just south of Glacier National Park.

Although not as essential as they once were, mining (especially gold, silver, zinc, platinum, and lead), cattle- and sheep-ranching, and agriculture are still very important to Montana's economy. Montana's farmers grow crops like wheat, barley, hay, and sugar beets.

History

Before Europeans first visited North America, Native Americans lived in Montana, on the edges of the plains, and would go onto the plains every once in a while to hunt buffalo. After Europeans brought the horse to America, many of these tribes moved out to live full-time on the plains as nomads, following the buffalo herds and hunting them year-round.

These nomadic peoples included the Cheyenne, the Gros Ventres (French for "Big Bellies"), the Arikara, the Crow, the Blackfoot, the Flatheads, and the Sioux (pronounced "soo"). Most of these tribes still live in Montana today. Their reservations dot the state, and Native American tribes are active participants in caring for the environment. These tribes all have their own governments, their own law codes, and their own police and fire departments!

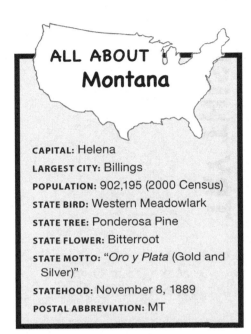

ALL ABOUT Montana

CAPITAL: Helena

LARGEST CITY: Billings

POPULATION: 902,195 (2000 Census)

STATE BIRD: Western Meadowlark

STATE TREE: Ponderosa Pine

STATE FLOWER: Bitterroot

STATE MOTTO: "*Oro y Plata* (Gold and Silver)"

STATEHOOD: November 8, 1889

POSTAL ABBREVIATION: MT

WORDS TO KNOW

Continental Divide

In the Rocky Mountains, which are the tallest point on our continent, the Continental Divide is the exact center point on the crest of the Rockies where water on one side of the mountains runs downhill and eventually enters the Atlantic Ocean and water on the other side of the mountains runs downhill and flows into the Pacific Ocean.

TRY THIS!

Make Your Own Continental Divide!

Make a mound of dirt in your backyard (get your parents' permission before you dig!). Try giving it a spine, like the top part of a tent. Now take your garden hose and pour a trickle of water along the spine, or crest, of your mountain range. What happens to the water? Does it run down one side, or the other, or both? If it runs down both, you're pouring the water right on top of the spine of your mountain range. So you've not only just made your own mountain range, you've just made your own continental divide!

Most of the state became the property of the United States after the Louisiana Purchase in 1803. That treaty gave the United States a claim to all of Montana up to the continental divide, but the western part of the state was still mostly unexplored at that time.

The Lewis and Clark expedition changed all that. They visited Montana both on the way to the Pacific coast and when returning to the east. They explored much of the state, and followed the Missouri to its source in the Rocky Mountains.

During the fifty years between Lewis and Clark visiting the region and the discovery of gold in Montana in the 1850s, there was a brisk fur trade going on. Companies such as the North West Fur Company and the American Fur Company established trading posts in the area, looking especially for beaver hides, which could be made into tall top hats.

Although Native Americans did most of the fur-trapping during this period, there were independent trappers from the east who competed with them. Many of these men lived among the local tribes and adopted their ways, including marrying and starting families with Native American women.

When gold was discovered in 1852, there was a mad rush into the region by people looking to get rich. These prospectors caused trouble with tribes like the Sioux and Cheyenne, who went to war several times to stop gold-seekers from invading their lands. During one of these wars, the Sioux lured soldiers under the command of Lt. Colonel George Armstrong Custer into an ambush in what is now eastern Montana, along the Little Bighorn River. Custer and all of his troopers (225 men) were killed within a thirty-minute period.

It was a huge victory for the Sioux and Cheyenne. However, within a year, the members of the tribes who had fought at Little Bighorn had almost all been captured and placed on a new reservation. By late 1877, even Sitting Bull, the Sioux chief and medicine man who had led the Sioux so skillfully, had fled north to Canada.

WYOMING: The Equality State

Geography and Industry

Wyoming is one of only two states in the Union that is a perfect rectangle. Can you guess the name of the other one? (It's Colorado, Wyoming's neighbor to the south.) Like Montana, Wyoming is part mountain state and part plains state. The Bighorn, Teton, and Wind River ranges of the Rocky Mountains all run through western Wyoming. So do the Laramie, Medicine Bow, and Absaroka ranges. Wyoming really is a mountain state!

The Powder River runs through the central part of the state, just east and south of where South Dakota's Black Hills run into Wyoming's northeastern corner. The mighty Snake River starts in Wyoming's western mountains and then runs into Idaho.

And there is the Yellowstone country. Lake Yellowstone is the largest lake in the state, and is the center of world-famous Yellowstone National Park, which is the world's first national park. Yellowstone National Park is home to a large herd of buffalo, lots of grizzly bears and wolves, and cougars and other predators that are endangered elsewhere. Also, Yellowstone is an area where there is a lot of volcanic activity, so there are many geysers and hot springs in the area.

Less than twenty miles south of Yellowstone National Park lies Grand Teton National Park, and it is gorgeous! Majestic peaks rise over the valley of the Snake River as the river makes its way into southern Idaho. The Continental Divide runs right through both of these amazing parks!

Wyoming's main economic venture is still cattle and sheep ranching. Just as the state has as many mountains and as much scenery as Montana and Colorado, it also has as much mineral wealth. Petroleum drilling is especially important.

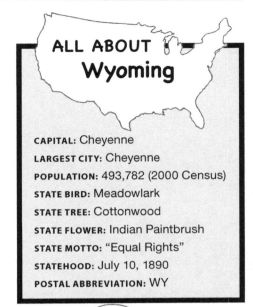

ALL ABOUT Wyoming

CAPITAL: Cheyenne
LARGEST CITY: Cheyenne
POPULATION: 493,782 (2000 Census)
STATE BIRD: Meadowlark
STATE TREE: Cottonwood
STATE FLOWER: Indian Paintbrush
STATE MOTTO: "Equal Rights"
STATEHOOD: July 10, 1890
POSTAL ABBREVIATION: WY

Fun Facts

OLD FAITHFUL NOT SO FAITHFUL?

Do you know about Old Faithful, the world-famous Yellowstone geyser? It was named Old Faithful because it was thought to be so reliable. Well, it's not! Old Faithful erupts in a tall cascade of water *on average* every sixty-five minutes, but it doesn't erupt nearly that regularly. The time between its eruptions can run anywhere from thirty to ninety minutes.

History

When the first French fur traders visited Wyoming, such tribes as the Crow, Cheyenne, Shoshone, and Sioux lived there. The Sioux lived in and around the Black Hills, the Crow lived in the south central part of the state, and the Cheyenne lived in both the north central and eastern part of the state (which is why the state's capital city, located in that region, is named after them). When white settlement began to push the Sioux out of their hunting grounds in South Dakota and the Black Hills region, they in turn pushed the Crow westward into the mountains.

The first American to visit what later became Wyoming was a former member of the Lewis and Clark expedition, a man named John Colter. Colter visited the Yellowstone region, saw its wonders, and told people about them when he returned east of the Mississippi. They laughed at him and thought he was lying. People back then talked about what they came to call Colter's Hell the same way that people today talk about Atlantis and Shangri-la.

The Oregon Trail runs east to west across Wyoming. It was the main route that people used to cross the continent and go to either Oregon or California before the coming of the railroads. In fact, in many places in Wyoming, you can still see the 150-year-old ruts left in the trail by the wheels of the settlers' wagons!

Wyoming became a territory in 1868. In 1869 women in Wyoming were the first w men in the United States to get the right to vote. Wyoming became a state in 1890, and in 1924 continued to be out in front in the struggle for women's rights, when Nellie Tayloe Ross was elected the first woman governor by any state (she was elected to finish out her deceased husband's term). Later on the same day, another woman, Miriam Ferguson, continued the trend by being elected governor of Texas!

WORDS TO KNOW

Suffrage

Unlike the way it sounds, the word "suffrage" has nothing to do with suffering. It means the right to vote in government elections. Not until 1919, less than 100 years ago, did every state give women the right to vote!

IDAHO: The Gem State

Geography and Industry

Idaho is a state full of contrasts: heavily forested northern mountains, semi-arid southern flatlands, mountain lakes, and the broad Snake River cutting a canyon across its own floodplain.

Along the narrow Idaho panhandle (which is less than fifty miles wide) in the northernmost part of the state, there are medium-sized mountain ranges such as the Cabinet Mountains, and gorgeous lakes such as Lake Coeur d'Alene, Priest Lake, and Lake Pend Oreille.

In the north and central parts of the state, Idaho is covered by high, rugged mountains such as Mount Borah, which is close to 13,000 feet high! The Bitterroot Range lies in the north, and in central Idaho are the towering Sawtooth Mountains. Between the Sawtooths and the broad Snake River Valley to the south are the smaller Salmon River Mountains.

The Snake River flows across southern Idaho from its source in northwestern Wyoming, to form part of the state's western border with Oregon. It has been dammed in a number of places so that its water could be used to irrigate dry land that is fertile but lacking in rainfall. This lets southern Idaho produce lots of agricultural products, especially potatoes, beans, peas, sugar beets, hay, and wheat. Cattle ranching also continues to be a very important industry in Idaho.

But agriculture is no longer the major money maker it once was, and mining in the state is on the decline. However, high-tech industries have become important, especially telecommunications companies and computer software companies.

One of Idaho's newest and fastest-growing industries is tourism. The state is lovely, and has several different types of outdoor recreation areas, including the skiing available at places like Sun Valley, and boating in places like Hells Canyon National Recreational Area.

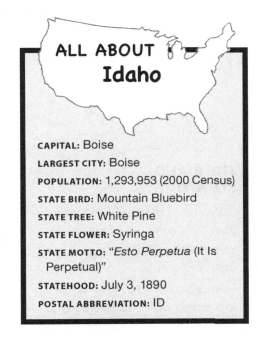

ALL ABOUT Idaho

CAPITAL: Boise
LARGEST CITY: Boise
POPULATION: 1,293,953 (2000 Census)
STATE BIRD: Mountain Bluebird
STATE TREE: White Pine
STATE FLOWER: Syringa
STATE MOTTO: "*Esto Perpetua* (It Is Perpetual)"
STATEHOOD: July 3, 1890
POSTAL ABBREVIATION: ID

Fun Facts

THE IDAHO POTATO

Do you like potatoes? Then more than likely you have eaten an Idaho potato, because Idaho leads the country in potato production. Many scientists think that potatoes do so well in southern Idaho because the climate is very similar to the climate in the Andes where potatoes evolved.

HELLS CANYON

Can you guess what the deepest canyon in North America is? It's not the Grand Canyon or Bryce Canyon—it's Hells Canyon in Idaho. At one point this canyon runs nearly 8,000 feet below the mountain peaks that surround it. You could stack five and half Empire State Buildings in a canyon that deep!

History

The first explorers of European descent to visit Idaho were the Lewis and Clark expedition, which followed the Snake River down to the Columbia and onward to the Pacific Ocean in 1805. At the time that Lewis and Clark entered Idaho, Native American tribes such as the Western Shoshone, Bannock, and Ute lived in the southern part of the state, the Nez Perce lived in western Idaho, and the Coeur d'Alene, Pend Oreille, and Kootenai lived in the north.

During the next forty years the only regular non–Native American visitors to Idaho were fur traders. They weren't the only whites to enter the region, though. The trading post at Fort Hall in southeastern Idaho was the point where the California Trail split off from the Oregon Trail and dipped south, headed toward northern California. None of the settlers who came west in those early years stayed in Idaho. They all pushed westward to either Oregon or California. That changed in the 1850s when gold was discovered in Idaho. Settlers poured into the region. Native Americans began to resist the settlement of their lands by whites seeking gold, government troops were called in, and the tribes were suppressed by the late 1850s.

The most famous Native American resistance to whites taking their land in Idaho occurred during 1876–77. The Nez Perce in western Idaho refused to move to a reservation, and fled their homes. They slipped into Montana, and almost made it into Canada, but were trapped and surrendered at Bear Paw Mountain, just a few miles south of the Canadian border. Chief Joseph and most of his people went to a reservation in eastern Washington. A few years later, many Nez Perce were able to return to their homes in Idaho.

Gold was discovered again in Idaho during the 1880s in Idaho's panhandle. The gold vein that miners found wasn't very big, but it led to the discovery of one of the largest veins of silver in the world. For the next 100 years, silver was mined out of several places in north Idaho. The mines ran dry in the early 1980s.

COLORADO: The Centennial State

Geography and Industry

Like Montana and Wyoming, Colorado has breathtaking scenery, and both high mountains and rolling plains. Eastern Colorado is part of the Great Plains, and is very hot and dry in the summer, then terribly cold during the winter. The other two geographic sections are the Rocky Mountains, which run from north to south through the central part of the state, and the Colorado Plateau, which is in the west.

Colorado's mountains are the tallest in the Rockies, and among the highest on the continent. In fact, Colorado has fifty-one of the eighty mountains in North America that are over 14,000 feet high!

The Rockies are made up of the Sangre de Cristos range, the Park Range, the Sawatch Mountains, the San Juan Mountains, and the Front Range. They are separated by wide basins called "parks." These include North Park, Estes Park, and South Park. Such mighty rivers as the Arkansas, the Red, the Colorado, both the North and the South Platte, and the Rio Grande all begin in Colorado's central mountain ranges. What's more, these mountains are covered with heavy forests of mostly conifers.

Western Colorado is a large plateau that is crossed by a number of canyons cut into the rock by fast-flowing rivers such as the Gunnison. Eastern Colorado is notable for its agriculture (cattle and sheep ranching especially), and the central region of the state is known for both high-tech (computer parts, software) and low-tech (metal production, electrical parts, etc.) industry. But the industry for which Colorado is world-famous is tourism.

Because it has so many outdoor recreational activities (hiking, biking, hunting, fishing, and skiing), Colorado has become a popular vacation spot. Resorts like Vail, Aspen, and Steamboat Springs attract people from all over the world.

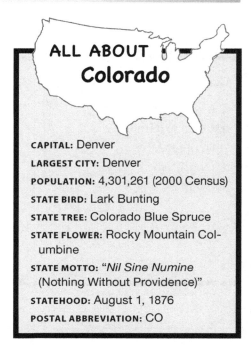

ALL ABOUT Colorado

CAPITAL: Denver

LARGEST CITY: Denver

POPULATION: 4,301,261 (2000 Census)

STATE BIRD: Lark Bunting

STATE TREE: Colorado Blue Spruce

STATE FLOWER: Rocky Mountain Columbine

STATE MOTTO: "*Nil Sine Numine* (Nothing Without Providence)"

STATEHOOD: August 1, 1876

POSTAL ABBREVIATION: CO

WORDS TO KNOW

Conifer

Conifers are trees that have needles instead of leaves, and drop cones instead of acorns when they're reproducing. Conifers are also evergreens, meaning that their needles stay on their limbs year-round.

WORDS TO KNOW

Centennial

The word centennial comes from a Latin phrase that means 100th anniversary.

History

Native Americans lived in the mesa country of southwestern Colorado for thousands of years before the coming of European explorers. First were the Basket Makers, who lived in the canyons of the mesa country. The Anasazi cliff-dwellers followed and built adobe houses along the walls of the same canyons that the Basket Makers had occupied before them.

At the time that American explorers such as Zebulon Pike (who discovered and named the famous Pike's Peak in 1806) visited Colorado, there were a number of different Native American tribes living on Colorado's plains. These tribes included the Arapaho, the Kiowa, the Southern Cheyenne, and the Ute.

During the 1840s, the plains tribes of Colorado went to war with white settlers to try to hold on to their lands. At the same time, the United States fought a war with Mexico. The Americans won both of these wars, and took much of northern Mexico, including what later became central and western Colorado, as part of the peace settlement of 1848.

As happened with many of the other Rocky Mountain states, Colorado experienced a huge explosion in population when gold was discovered near the present-day site of Denver in the early 1850s. The rush of gold prospectors and other settlers into the region pushed the local Native American tribes to war several times over the next twenty years.

White settlers in the region tried to organize a territory that they called Jefferson in 1859, but Congress refused to recognize them. So they acted illegally as a territorial government for nearly two years, until Congress finally passed a law that organized Colorado as a territory. Coloradans tried twice to become a state before Congress finally recognized the territory as one in 1876. Because this year was also the 100th anniversary of the signing of the Declaration of Independence, Colorado became known as the Centennial State.

UTAH: The Beehive State

Geography and Industry

Western Utah is a dry lake bed. Thousands of years ago, it was the bottom of the massive Lake Bonneville. The Great Salt Lake is all that is left of this ancient lake. Central Utah is a long, narrow, fertile valley. Most of Utah's cities lie in this corridor. Eastern Utah is very mountainous in the north, and has a network of deep, beautiful canyons. These include the world-famous Bryce Canyon and Zion Canyon. Many of these formations were created by the Colorado River, which flows northeast to southwest across the southeastern corner of the state.

There are many other natural wonders to see in Utah. They include Canyonlands and Arches (both national parks), and national monuments such as Golden Spike, Dinosaur, Grand Staircase-Escalantre, and Rainbow Bridge. There are ancient cliff dwellings in Capitol Reef National Park.

Mining is a very important part of Utah's economy. There is a lot of copper, gold, magnesium, and petroleum. Other metals, such as silver, lead, tin, and uranium, are mined there as well.

Because the terrain is so dry and rocky, the amount of land used for agriculture is very small. In the land that is usable as farmland, barley, corn, hay, and wheat are grown. Cattle, sheep, and poultry are also raised in large quantities.

Tourism is a growing industry in Utah. Not only do the canyons and rock formations of the east and the southern deserts draw many visitors every year, but so does the world-class skiing in places such as Park City, which is in the Wasatch Mountains in the northeastern part of the state.

History

Like neighboring states Colorado, New Mexico, and Arizona, Utah was occupied over a thousand years ago by cliff-dwellers who built in Utah's canyons using adobe. By the time the

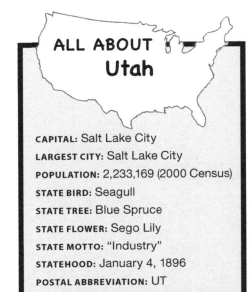

ALL ABOUT
Utah

CAPITAL: Salt Lake City
LARGEST CITY: Salt Lake City
POPULATION: 2,233,169 (2000 Census)
STATE BIRD: Seagull
STATE TREE: Blue Spruce
STATE FLOWER: Sego Lily
STATE MOTTO: "Industry"
STATEHOOD: January 4, 1896
POSTAL ABBREVIATION: UT

Spanish visited the region, the major Native American tribes living in Utah were the Western Shoshone, the Ute, and the Paiute.

Trappers like Jim Bridger worked throughout Utah, looking for beaver in the early 1800s. Bridger was the first white man to see the Great Salt Lake (in 1824). He was also the guide who led Brigham Young's first Mormon wagon trains to northern Utah.

Utah and the Mormons

The Mormons were established as a religious sect in the early 1800s by Joseph Smith, in upstate New York. As they gained in numbers, they moved several times, relocating to Ohio, then to Missouri, and after that to Illinois.

Later, Brigham Young was responsible for the Mormon migration to the far west. He hired Jim Bridger to lead the way. They arrived in the valley of the Great Salt Lake on July 24, 1847.

By 1850, all of Utah and part of what later became Nevada was designated by the U.S. government as the Utah Territory. However, it took nearly half a century and the threat of civil war before Utah became a state. This was mostly because the Mormons practiced polygamy, which means a man marrying more than one wife. Polygamy was illegal in the United States, but Mormons practiced it as part of their religion. In 1858 they had a series of skirmishes with U.S. troops sent to the territory to remove Brigham Young as governor. James Buchanan replaced Young as governor, but Young remained head of the Mormon Church.

A Transportation Revolution

On May 10, 1869, Leland Stanford, a California railroad owner, drove the ceremonial "golden" spike in the first transcontinental railroad tracks. The spike was driven in at Promontory Point in the northern part of Utah. With the opening of the railroad, travel between the west coast and the east coast went from taking months to taking days.

Fun Facts

THE GOLDEN SPIKE NOT SO GOLDEN?

The only problem is that the "golden" spike wasn't really golden! It's true! Pure gold is far too soft to be pounded into a wooden railroad tie with a hammer. So the builders used a spike that was made of an alloy of different metals, including gold, and covered in gold plating.

Sweeping from the borders of the southern plains all the way to the Pacific Ocean, the states of the Southwest are made up of vast deserts, high mountains, large rivers, and magnificent forests. This is the region that houses the mighty Grand Canyon and the ancient Sequoia trees of northern California, the wide Mojave Desert, and both the high Rocky Mountains and the rugged Sierra Nevada.

The Southwest has states with small populations, such as New Mexico, and the state with the largest population, California. It is both incredibly rural, with thousands of square miles where no human lives, and also incredibly urban. Orange County in California, for example, has more people living there than live on the entire continent of Australia!

There are rivers such as the Rio Grande, the Colorado, and the Sacramento running through the Southwest, and they drain millions of square miles of land into the Gulf of Mexico, the Gulf of California, and the Pacific Ocean. The Pacific Ocean runs along the western edge of the region, and on that coast there are fine natural harbors such as San Francisco Bay, Drake's Bay, and San Diego Harbor, to name just a few.

NEW MEXICO: Land of Enchantment

Geography and Industry

New Mexico straddles the Continental Divide in the western part of the state. Eastern New Mexico is covered by dry plains that get very little water. The Rio Grande River runs south from its source in Colorado through the state, and forms neighboring Texas's long border with Mexico. The mountain ranges that form spurs of the Rockies include the Sangre de Cristos, which rise to heights of nearly 14,000 feet in places.

ALL ABOUT New Mexico

CAPITAL: Santa Fe

LARGEST CITY: Albuquerque

POPULATION: 1,819,046 (2000 Census)

STATE BIRD: Roadrunner

STATE TREE: Pinon

STATE FLOWER: Yucca

STATE MOTTO: "*Crescit Eundo* (It Grows as It Goes)"

STATEHOOD: January 6, 1912

POSTAL ABBREVIATION: NM

Because water is so scarce in New Mexico, there is little fertile land. The land that is available is used mostly for grazing. Cattle and sheep raising are still major industries in New Mexico.

There are very few fruits and vegetables grown in New Mexico aside from hay, onions, potatoes, and grapes grown in the Rio Grande Valley. These grapes are used to make wine. In fact, New Mexico was the first place in the United States where vineyards were planted and grown, going back to 1610!

Parts of New Mexico are made up of limestone bluffs that are the remains of an ancient undersea reef. These bluffs have been eroded by wind and rain, and have been sculpted into gorgeous and strangely shaped mesas. Underground, the limestone in this region has been eroded by groundwater to form huge limestone caves, complete with stalactites and stalagmites!

Like other states with the Rocky Mountains running through them, New Mexico is rich in minerals. These include ore like copper, manganese, silver, tin, and uranium. Turquoise is found in the state in large quantities. There is a lot of natural gas in New Mexico, but not much petroleum or coal.

One out of every four people who hold a job in New Mexico works for the U.S. government. There are many military bases in the state, and some national observatories (places where scientists use telescopes to study the stars). Los Alamos, where the first atomic bombs were designed and built, is still a working government laboratory.

New Mexico gets millions of tourists every year. Aztec Ruins National Monument (which marks Pueblo ruins, not Aztec ones, despite the name!) and Carlsbad Caverns National Park are just a couple of the most popular places for tourists to go in the state. In the north, the very old city of Taos is the site of a number of art festivals that also draw lots of visitors every year.

WORDS TO KNOW

Stalactite/Stalagmite

What's the difference between stalactites and stalagmites, the rock deposits that look like icicles in underground caves? A stalactite hangs from the ceiling, and is formed by limestone deposits left behind by groundwater dripping from the ceiling toward the floor. Some of the limestone gets left behind on the floor where the water drips, and builds up into formations called stalagmites.

CARLSBAD CAVERNS

The Carlsbad Cavern system contains over eighty different caves, including Lechuguilla Cave, which is the deepest cave in the United States! It was discovered in 1986, and has been measured down to a depth of nearly 1,567 feet (That is deeper than a 110-story skyscraper!). It has not been completely explored yet, so it might be even deeper!

Spanish Explorers

As was the case with most of the states in the Southwest, the Spanish were the first Europeans to visit New Mexico. Before they came to New Mexico during the 1500s, the land was occupied by a flourishing Pueblo civilization that had been in place farming the river bottoms of the Rio Grande and other rivers such as the Pecos.

The first Spaniards to visit the region were the conquistadors who followed Captain General Francisco Vasquez de Coronado north from Mexico in 1540. Coronado was looking for the mythical Seven Cities of Cibola, which were supposedly so full of gold that the natives paved their streets with it. Although he rode all the way into what is now western Kansas, all Coronado found were Pueblo farmers and plains tribes.

He did, however, leave a lasting impression on the Native Americans of New Mexico. Coronado and his men were needlessly cruel to the tribes they encountered. As a result, over and over again during the following two centuries, the Pueblos and the Apaches (who lived in western New Mexico and what is now Arizona) fought very hard against the Spanish as they tried to establish a colony and a mission system.

History

In 1609 a colonial government was established at Taos, which is one of the oldest continuously inhabited European-built cities in North America. By 1680, the Spanish colonial government had again so angered the local Native Americans that the tribes once again went to war. This time, things were different; the Spanish lost, and they had to flee from New Mexico. The Pueblos and Apaches were able to keep the Spanish out of New Mexico for over twelve years!

Just over a century later, Mexico won its independence from Spain. That year New Mexico (which included what is now Arizona) became a Mexican province. The Mexicans were interested in trade with their neighbors to the north, and encouraged American traders to come to Mexico to do business. By 1822 (a year after Mexico became independent), American traders had established what we now call the Santa Fe Trail, which ran from what is now Kansas down to Santa Fe in New Mexico.

In 1846 Mexico and the United States went to war over Mexico's northern provinces. Mexico lost, and part of the result was that New Mexico became an American territory. New Mexico became a state in 1912, just ahead of Arizona, which had made up the other half of New Mexico territory when it first joined the United States!

ARIZONA: The Grand Canyon State

Geography and Industry

When you think of Arizona, what do you think of? The Grand Canyon? Lots and lots of desert, and rocks, and maybe a few mountains? Well, Arizona has all of those things, but it has so much more! There are forests and large rivers in Arizona, and the state has farms that produce lots of food.

The northern part of the state, where the Grand Canyon is, is part of the Colorado Plateau, and is very rugged and mountainous. It's also covered in several places, including part of the southern rim of the Grand Canyon, with evergreen forests, especially Ponderosa Pines. The Colorado River system (including the Little Colorado River) runs both through the Grand Canyon, which it has carved over millions of years, and through the north central and northwestern parts of the state.

WORDS TO KNOW

Pueblo

The word "pueblo" has a couple of different meanings. It comes from the type of adobe (mud brick) buildings built by several different cultures in the Southwest. It has also come to stand as a collective name for the cultures (the Anasazi, the Zuni, the Hopi, and so on) who built with it. Adobe is still used as a building material to this day in the region!

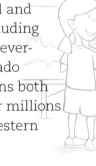

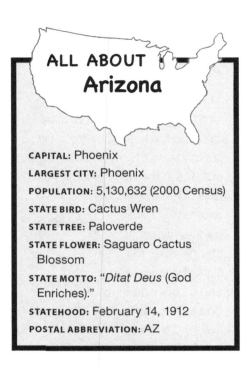

ALL ABOUT Arizona

CAPITAL: Phoenix

LARGEST CITY: Phoenix

POPULATION: 5,130,632 (2000 Census)

STATE BIRD: Cactus Wren

STATE TREE: Paloverde

STATE FLOWER: Saguaro Cactus Blossom

STATE MOTTO: *"Ditat Deus* (God Enriches)."

STATEHOOD: February 14, 1912

POSTAL ABBREVIATION: AZ

The southern part of the state is mostly extremely dry desert plains with a few mountains rising on either side of the Gila River valley. The Gila is a large river that runs east to west across the state and empties into the Colorado.

Like many of the western states, Arizona has a lot of beautiful scenery, so tourism is a major industry in the state. In addition to the Grand Canyon, there are other popular areas such as the Painted Desert, the Native American pueblo ruins at places like Canyon de Chelly in the northeastern part of the state, the Petrified Forest National Park, and the Mogollon Rim.

Just like in the other western states, cattle-ranching and crop-raising are very important industries in Arizona. The main crops raised are broccoli, cauliflower, cotton, lettuce, and sorghum.

History

Before the Spanish began exploring the region during the sixteenth century, there were many different tribes of Native Americans living in what is now Arizona. An early culture we know as the Hohokum ("hoh-HOH-kem") lived in pit houses dug into the earth and covered with thatched mud roofs. They were farmers who irrigated their fields with water from neighboring rivers. They flourished for nearly 1,000 years, from 500 A.D. to 1450 A.D.

The Spanish explorer Francisco Vasquez de Coronado visited Arizona, discovering the Grand Canyon in 1540. Although many Spanish soldiers came to the region over the next 100 years, they were exploring—looking for gold, not interested in settling the area. The first Spanish visitors to settle permanently in Arizona were Spanish priests who came as missionaries to convert the local Native Americans to Christianity. These friars established the first permanent settlements near Nogales and Tucson in 1692.

Mexico briefly controlled Arizona before losing it as part of the Mexican Cession to the United States in 1848. In 1853, the United States bought more territory from Mexico and added it to the New Mexico Territory. This land was south of the Gila River, and the United States hoped to build a railroad through it out to California. It later became part first of the Arizona Territory (1863), then of the state of Arizona.

During the forty-nine years that Arizona was a territory, it had quite a colorful history. Several tribes of the Apache nation maintained an on-again, off-again war with the U.S. government. Such great Apache leaders as Mangas Coloradas (whose name in Spanish means "Red Sleeves," referring to the color of his favorite shirt), Cochise, and Geronimo fought the U.S. Cavalry to a standstill for decades.

The Apache were skilled at the art of guerilla warfare. They struck in one place, and faded away like smoke. They would also raid a site and then slip across the border into Mexico, where they knew the soldiers weren't allowed to chase them. Even after they agreed to move to reservations, many young Apache braves would slip off the reservation, raid several settlers' farms, and then slip back on to the reservation before their absence had been noticed. The government's solution was to remove such warriors as the great Geronimo from Arizona and send them to a reservation in Oklahoma. (Geronimo was eventually sent all the way to Florida!)

Beginning in the 1870s, large copper mines sprang up in the hills around Tucson. In 1877, silver was discovered in Cochise's old stomping grounds in the Dragoon Mountains near Tombstone, which was a boom town east of Tucson. Miners flooded into the area, and so did gamblers, saloon-keepers, gun-fighters, and other people right out of a Western movie!

Arizona became a state in 1912, just a few months after neighboring New Mexico. From 1940 to 1960, Arizona's population increased by 100 percent, the fastest growth-rate in American history! To this day, people are moving to the state for its warm climate and mild winters.

WORDS TO KNOW

Guerilla

"Guerilla" is a Spanish word that refers to a type of warfare where the people fighting specialize in hit-and-run raids, rather than acquiring, occupying, and holding enemy territory.

Fun Facts

THE MOST FAMOUS GUNFIGHT

People such as the Earp brothers, led by the famous Wyatt Earp, came to Arizona looking to get rich quick. The Earps eventually got into a power struggle with another local family, the Clantons. This power struggle led to the most famous gunfight in western history: the gunfight at the OK Corral!

ALL ABOUT
Nevada

CAPITAL: Carson City

LARGEST CITY: Las Vegas

POPULATION: 1,998,257 (2000 Census)

STATE BIRD: Mountain Bluebird

STATE TREE: Single-leaf Pinon

STATE FLOWER: Sagebrush

STATE MOTTO: "All for Our Country."

STATEHOOD: October 31, 1864

POSTAL ABBREVIATION: NV

NEVADA: The Silver State

Geography and Industry

Within its borders, Nevada has high mountains (the Sierra Nevada, which run along its border with California) and a couple of huge deserts (the Great Basin, which is located in the eastern and central portions of the state, and the Mojave, which runs across the southern tip). In the northern part of the state are some high plateaus, which have the state's available grazing land. Nevada is poor in water—it is the driest state in the Union—but wealthy in minerals.

Mining is a very important industry in Nevada. Nevada's mines produce more gold, mercury, and silver than those of any other state. There are copper and oil deposits in the state as well. What few crops that are grown in this harsh, dry climate include hay to feed the livestock bred in the north.

Nevada's climate varies widely between the state's different regions. In the mountains of the northwest, the winters are very cold. In the southern tip, near Las Vegas, the summer heat gets so hot that it takes your breath away!

Like many other western states, Nevada relies heavily on tourism as well as on its mineral wealth. Reno in the northwest and Las Vegas in the south are very popular tourist destinations, attracting millions of visitors per year. Lake Tahoe, which is close to Reno, is also one of the most popular skiing vacation destinations in the world. On the Colorado River, which forms part of Nevada's border with Arizona in the south, Hoover Dam was built during the 1930s. It is one of the largest dams in the United States and generates inexpensive hydroelectricity to power the bright lights of neighboring Las Vegas.

History

Before white settlement in the mid-nineteenth century, Nevada was relatively empty. Members of the Paiute and Ute tribes lived in the north and the Great Basin. From the 1820s through the 1840s, a number of fur traders and explorers like Peter Skene Ogden of Canada's North West Fur Company, the independent American trapper Jedidiah Smith, and U.S. Army Captain John C. Fremont visited the region and explored it extensively.

Also beginning in the 1840s, two wagon-train trails were blazed across Nevada. One trail crossed the Sierra Nevada in the north, and another passed through the small town of Las Vegas in the south, both connecting the American states in the east to the California gold fields on the Pacific coast.

At first very few settlers stopped in Nevada. Most of them just kept heading for California. The Comstock strike in northern Nevada in 1858 changed all of that. The Comstock Lode turned out to be the richest silver strike in American history, and it attracted so many people so quickly to work claims in the Sierra Nevada that what had been an empty part of the Utah Territory just a few short years before became the Nevada Territory in 1861, and the state of Nevada in 1864.

Hoover Dam

By the turn of the twentieth century, times were tough in Nevada, because silver prices were down and most of the gold mines in the state weren't producing as much as they had previously. During the early twentieth century, the U.S. government began to take a big part in developing the state's economy. First the government funded the building of Hoover Dam (which was finished in 1936) and then it decided to make Nevada the major site for its nuclear testing.

WORDS TO KNOW

Lode

A lode is a deposit of any sort of metal that is connected and continuous. These are sometimes also called veins.

Hoover Dam brought cheap electric power to neighboring Las Vegas. Thanks to this, and to Nevada's new laws that legalized gambling, Las Vegas began to attract tourists away from places in the east where gambling was legal, such as Atlantic City.

Another result of Hoover Dam's construction across the powerful Colorado River was the creation of Lake Mead. Boating, camping, water-skiing, and fishing in the waters of Lake Mead are all popular outdoor activities in southern Nevada.

Lastly, Hoover Dam has helped divert countless tons of water from the Colorado River and send it to irrigate much of the fertile (but arid) farmland of neighboring southern California. As a result, California is one of the biggest producers of fruits and vegetables in the world today!

CALIFORNIA: The Golden State

Geography and Industry

California is so big that it could practically be a country on its own. It's true! Even though it's not the largest state in the Union (Alaska and Texas are larger), it is the third-largest area-wise, and it does have the largest population of any state. What's more, if California were an independent country, this state's economy is so huge that it would be listed among the ten largest economies among the nations of the world!

California occupies 800 miles along the American Pacific coast, which is over half of America's western coastline. It is long and thin, measuring around 250 miles wide, and bordered on the east by the mighty Sierra Nevada Mountains in the northeast and the Colorado River in the southeast.

In many ways California is one huge valley. Bordered in the east by the Sierra Nevada, its west coast is covered by a long range of low-lying mountains known as the Coast Range. Running for hundreds of miles along the central part of the

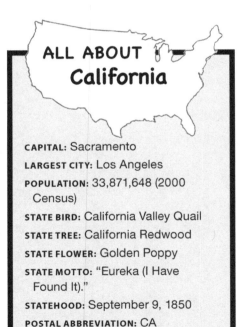

ALL ABOUT California

CAPITAL: Sacramento

LARGEST CITY: Los Angeles

POPULATION: 33,871,648 (2000 Census)

STATE BIRD: California Valley Quail

STATE TREE: California Redwood

STATE FLOWER: Golden Poppy

STATE MOTTO: "Eureka (I Have Found It)."

STATEHOOD: September 9, 1850

POSTAL ABBREVIATION: CA

state in between these two mountain ranges is the Central Valley. Two large river systems, the Sacramento and the San Joaquin, run through this valley and provide water for one of the most fertile areas in the world.

Although other states are known mostly as farming states, none produces more fruits and vegetables than California. California grows more almonds, broccoli, carrots, lettuce, onions, strawberries, and tomatoes than any other state. It also leads the country in dairy products. So more milk, cheese, and eggs come from California than from anywhere else in the nation! Cotton, grapes, flowers, and oranges are other important crops grown in California.

California doesn't just lead the country in food production, though. It has a lot of high-tech industry in the state, especially in the north, where part of the San Francisco Bay area is known as Silicon Valley because of all of the computer parts it produces (silicon is a mineral used in making computers). It is also a leading manufacturer of everything from appliances and car parts to airplane parts. During World War II, southern California's manufacturing industry blossomed because of defense contracts to build planes, tanks, jeeps, cars, and so on for the American forces fighting in the war.

History

Before the arrival of the Spanish in the mid-sixteenth century, there were many Native Americans living in California's mild climate. These groups weren't really tribes, but small family groups. These people were skilled basket weavers, and their art survives down to the present day. Most of them spoke dialects of Native American languages such as Chumash, Coastanoan, and Digueno.

The Spanish claimed all of the North American west coast, and explored it far north of what is now California during the

Fun Facts

THE HIGH AND THE LOW OF IT

Did you know that both the highest and the lowest points in the continental United States are in California? Mount Whitney, which measures 14,494 feet, is less than ninety miles from Death Valley, which is the lowest point at 282 feet below sea level. Death Valley has also had the highest recorded temperature in the United States at 134 degrees Fahrenheit in 1913!

sixteenth, seventeenth, and eighteenth centuries. They finally began to colonize north of Mexico, moving into what is now San Diego in the province they called Alta California (upper California) to differentiate it from the established province of Baja California (lower California) in the year 1769.

The Spanish set up a mission system that allowed the Catholic Church to hold the land of the local Native Americans "in trust," and cultivate it, using the Native Americans themselves as their labor. So these Mission Indians (as they came to be known) had their land taken from them, and then they were herded into the mission settlements and forced to work the very land that was stolen from them for no pay!

After Mexico declared independence from Spain, the Mexican government seized the mission lands and freed the Mission Indians from their slavery. But the Mexican period in Alta California did not last long. Even before Mexico lost California at the end of the Mexican-American War in 1848, Americans had begun to immigrate to California in droves.

During the Mexican War, a young army captain sent west to map the American possessions in the Rockies led his exploring expedition to northern California in order to see what good he could do for his country there. His name was John C. Fremont, and he succeeded in stirring up American settlers (as well as many Californians of Mexican descent), resulting in the Bear Flag Revolt. The Americans and many Californios (Californians of Mexican descent) threw out the occupying Mexican troops. A republic was formed just long enough to vote to join the United States. California became a free state (a state where slavery was outlawed) in 1850.

One of the reasons why there were enough Americans living in California for it to become a state in 1850 was that gold had been discovered in northern California at a place called Sutter's Fort. The people who crossed the continent intending to get rich quickly in California became known as Forty-Niners because the California Gold Rush began in 1849.

HAWAII: The Aloha State

Geography and Industry

Stretching over 1,000 miles from southeast to northwest in the central Pacific Ocean, the islands that make up the state of Hawaii were built up over centuries by volcanic activity on the ocean floor. There are still several active volcanoes in the Hawaiian Islands today. These mountains include Haleakala on the island of Maui, and Mauna Kea and Mauna Loa on the island of Hawaii. The largest islands in the group are Hawaii, Lanai, Kahoolawe, Kauai, Maui, Molokai, Niihau, and Oahu.

The "big" island of Hawaii is both the largest and the "youngest" of the islands in the group. Oahu has the most people living there, and is the most popular tourist destination, with Waikiki Beach, and Waimea Bay drawing thousands of visitors per year.

Tourism is Hawaii's chief industry, although specialty foods sugar cane and pineapples are grown there in abundance. There is so much to do in Hawaii: for starters, there's skiing on the mountains of the Big Island, snorkeling along the many coral reefs that have sprung up around the islands, surfing, whale-watching off of Maui, and watching "cowboys" rounding up Hawaii's other big food export, cattle!

Another popular Hawaiian recreational activity is fishing. Whether it is surf fishing from the beach, or sport fishing out on the blue waters surrounding the islands, fishing is not just a recreational industry—for some people, it's a way of life. In fact, fish and fishing are so important in Hawaii that it's the only state to have its own official state fish!

History

Hawaii was first settled by Polynesian settlers from the South Pacific around A.D. 400 For over a thousand years afterward, the natives of the individual islands fought each other, Oahu against Kauai and so on.

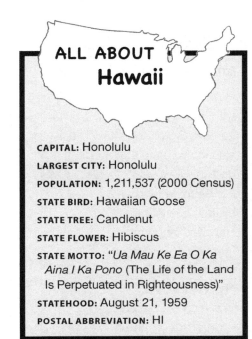

ALL ABOUT Hawaii

CAPITAL: Honolulu

LARGEST CITY: Honolulu

POPULATION: 1,211,537 (2000 Census)

STATE BIRD: Hawaiian Goose

STATE TREE: Candlenut

STATE FLOWER: Hibiscus

STATE MOTTO: "*Ua Mau Ke Ea O Ka Aina I Ka Pono* (The Life of the Land Is Perpetuated in Righteousness)"

STATEHOOD: August 21, 1959

POSTAL ABBREVIATION: HI

Fun Facts

PINEAPPLES— NOT A HAWAIIAN FRUIT?

Did you know that pineapples are not native to Hawaii? It's true! Pineapples evolved in the jungles of northeastern South America, in what is now Guyana. They were first imported to Hawaii in the late nineteenth century, and they quickly became a popular cash crop!

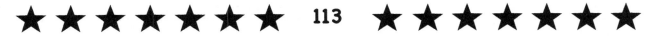

WORDS TO KNOW

Humuhumunukunukuapuaa

Hawaii is the only state in the Union with an official state fish, and its name is bigger than it is! The fish is also known as a triggerfish. However, it is better known by its name in the Hawaiian language: humuhumunukunukuapuaa ("hooh-mooh-hooh-mooh-nooh-kooh-nooh-kooh-ah-pooh-ah-ah").

The first Europeans to visit the islands were the crew of the British naval vessel the *HMS Discovery*, under the command of the famous explorer Captain James Cook, in 1778. Soon after Cook's expedition revealed Hawaii's existence to the outside world, American whalers began to visit Hawaii. They were followed by Christian missionaries in the early 1800s.

In 1810 King Kamehameha I ("kah-MAY-uh-MAY-uh") united the islands and established the Kingdom of Hawaii. His family ruled the islands until 1872, when his grandson, King Kamehameha V, died. The royal family tried for decades to resist the influence of American missionaries and businessmen (who came to Hawaii to make money from the booming sugar trade), with little success.

In 1893 a bloodless revolution deposed Queen Liliuokalani ("li-LEE-uh-oh-kah-LAH-nee"), the last monarch of the Kingdom of Hawaii. John L. Stephens, the American minister (ambassador) to Hawaii, was appointed the head of the new government, and declared Hawaii a U.S. protectorate (meaning that it became a protected territory of the United States).

Interestingly enough, American president Grover Cleveland refused to sign the order annexing Hawaii! He correctly believed that most native Hawaiians didn't support annexation, and he didn't want the United States to be a political bully.

The next U.S. president, William McKinley, supported American annexation of Hawaii, and he got his wish in 1898. Hawaii became a territory in 1900. Hawaii's fine port of Pearl Harbor became a major U.S. naval base over the next few decades. In fact, Pearl Harbor was so important to the U.S. military that when the Japanese decided to go to war with the United States in December of 1941, the first thing it did was bomb the harbor. The Japanese Navy launched a surprise attack against Pearl Harbor, sinking several of the battleships of the U.S. Pacific fleet and killing over 2,000 American civilians and military personnel.

Hawaii became the fiftieth state in 1959, less than eight months after Alaska became the forty-ninth state in January of that same year.

CHAPTER 10

THE NORTHWEST, DISTRICT OF COLUMBIA, AND PUERTO RICO

The Pacific Northwest runs from the foothills of the Rocky Mountains to the coast of the Pacific Ocean, and from northern California to the Canadian border, then onward to the Arctic and the massive state of Alaska.

The Pacific Northwest is a region of massive rivers and high mountains, and it has the only non-jungle rain forest in the United States. Although many people think of the Pacific Northwest as a place where the sun never shines and it never stops raining, there are parts of the region that are as dry as any desert.

OREGON: The Beaver State

Geography and Industry

Oregon has three major mountain ranges crossing it: the low-lying Coastal Range, which runs along the shore of the Pacific Ocean; the rugged Cascade Range (including the gorgeous Mount Hood and the picturesque Mount Batchelor), which goes north to south through the west-central part of the state; and the Blue and Wallowa Mountains, which run from northeastern Oregon into neighboring Washington and Idaho.

Nestled between the Coastal Range and the Cascades is the incredibly fertile Willamette River Valley. The eastern and central parts of the state are arid plateau land, which receives very little rainfall but under irrigation has become very productive farmland in many places. This part of Oregon is ideal grazing land, and the state has a huge cattle industry.

Oregon's major agricultural products include beans, broccoli, cherries, hay, onions, pears, peppermint, strawberries, and wheat. Oregon has also begun to produce wine locally during the past couple of decades, made from grapes grown in the state's arid central region.

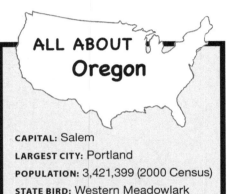

ALL ABOUT
Oregon

CAPITAL: Salem
LARGEST CITY: Portland
POPULATION: 3,421,399 (2000 Census)
STATE BIRD: Western Meadowlark
STATE TREE: Douglas Fir
STATE FLOWER: Oregon Grape
STATE MOTTO: "The Union"
STATEHOOD: February 14, 1859
POSTAL ABBREVIATION: OR

Oregon has been called a sportsperson's paradise for many good reasons, including skiing in the Cascades; fishing, kayaking, and boating on the ocean and in the state's many lakes, streams, and rivers; and hiking in and around Oregon's many mountain ranges.

Because there is so much to see and do in Oregon, tourism has become a major industry in the state. The state's beaches are some of the most beautiful in the world, and every inch of them is public land, which by law cannot be sold. In southeastern Oregon, the Sea Lion Caves are popular with tourists, as is Crater Lake, which is at the center of Crater Lake National Park.

History

Before the first Europeans began visiting the region during the sixteenth century, there were many different tribes of Native Americans living in what is now Oregon. The Nez Perce lived in eastern Oregon, in the Wallowa Valley. The Modoc lived in dry lava beds of southern Oregon. The Cayuse and Umatilla lived in eastern and northern Oregon. And the Chinook lived and traded along the Columbia River all the way from its mouth up to the present-day site of Portland, Oregon's largest city.

After Captain Robert Gray of Boston, Massachusetts, located the mouth of the Columbia (which he named after his ship, the *Columbia Rediviva*) in 1792, other ships began to visit the region. The Chinooks began to act as middlemen who traded furs from tribes living farther up the river for the trade goods (blankets, glass beads, guns, and so on) that these ships brought.

The first permanent settlement in what is now Oregon was the establishment in 1811 of the fur-trading post of Astoria on the present site of the city of Astoria, Oregon. The post

Fun Facts

CRATER LAKE

Nearly 7,000 years ago, an 11,000-foot-high mountain stood on the spot today occupied by Crater Lake. Around 4850 B.C., that mountain erupted with the force of several hundred nuclear warheads. When the mountain blew up, it left behind a smoking crater that filled with water over the course of several centuries. And that's how Crater Lake came to be.

WORDS TO KNOW

The Oregon Trail

Established in the early 1830s, the Oregon Trail began in Independence, Missouri, crossed the Great Plains, the Rocky Mountains, the Great Basin, and finally the Cascade Range, ending in the farmland of the Willamette Valley. Although it is no longer used today, there are places along the trail where the wagon ruts made over 150 years ago can still be seen!

was founded by members of the American Fur Company, and they named the post after the company's owner, New York's John Jacob Astor. During the War of 1812, the post was seized by the British, and for the next thirty years Americans competed with British subjects for control of the Oregon Country.

Oregon at the time ran from California in the south up the west coast nearly to Alaska in the north, and from the Continental Divide in the east to the Pacific Ocean in the west. Parts of the present-day states of Wyoming and Montana, as well as all of the states of Oregon, Washington, and Idaho, and the entire Canadian province of British Columbia were included in this vast territory.

In 1818, and again in 1842, Great Britain and the United States agreed to a joint occupation of the Oregon Country by their citizens, and to no active military units in the area. In the 1830s, American settlers began to cross the continent by wagon train, coming all the way to the Willamette Valley to settle and establish farms. These early settlers established the Oregon Trail, which thousands followed afterward.

In 1846 the United States and Great Britain split the Oregon Country along the Forty-Ninth Parallel. They did so peacefully, without a shot being fired. The American side became the Oregon Territory, and remained so until Oregon became a state in 1859.

Scared Silly

These two old miners are trying to tell you a joke. The answer is the name of a kind of town found in many western states. In fact, the state of Oregon has more than 1,000 of them! Figure out the miners' secret language so you can laugh along with them.

HINT: Look for a common word that is repeated over and over.

ALL ABOUT Washington

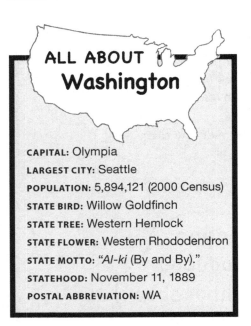

CAPITAL: Olympia

LARGEST CITY: Seattle

POPULATION: 5,894,121 (2000 Census)

STATE BIRD: Willow Goldfinch

STATE TREE: Western Hemlock

STATE FLOWER: Western Rhododendron

STATE MOTTO: "*Al-ki* (By and By)."

STATEHOOD: November 11, 1889

POSTAL ABBREVIATION: WA

WORDS TO KNOW

Geoduck

The word "geoduck" ("GOO-ee-duk") comes from a local Native American phrase that means "dig deep." A geoduck is not a bird; it's a huge species of clam that can be found only in and around Washington's Puget Sound. These clams have shells that only measure about six inches around, but they can weigh as much as twenty pounds!

WASHINGTON: The Evergreen State

Geography and Industry

Washington is a large western state that has the Columbia River running north to south through most of it. Then the river turns westward and runs along Washington's southern border with Oregon, all the way to the sea. Puget ("PYOO-jit") Sound, the largest saltwater inlet on the west coast, runs through western Washington and separates the large Olympic Peninsula from the rest of the state.

The jagged, picturesque Olympic Mountains rise on that peninsula, and within Olympic National Park lies almost all of the only rainforest in the continental United States. The east side of Puget Sound is bordered by the very tall Cascade Mountains. They reach their greatest height at the summit of Mount Rainier, which lies just southeast of the state's largest city of Seattle, and rises up to a little over 14,000 feet.

The Cascades block warm wet ocean air from reaching the state's interior (and are the cause for a lot of the rain that falls around Puget Sound). As a result, the Columbia River Basin, which stretches from the eastern Cascades to the foothills of the Rockies in the eastern part of the state, is pretty dry. Large rivers such as the Spokane, the Wenatchee, the Yakima, and the Snake all flow into the Columbia in this region.

Because the soil of the area is made up of large deposits of nutrient-rich volcanic dirt, water from these rivers used for irrigation of the dry land has turned Washington's desert area into a garden. Such crops as apples, pears, cherries, wheat, barley, hops, and grapes grow in such abundance here that they are a major export for the state.

In addition to all of the fruits and vegetables grown for sale in this state, there is a large livestock industry (including beef cattle and sheep, and especially poultry). On top of that, Washington's position on the northwest coast, near some of the north Pacific's richest fishing grounds, ensures that it produces a lot of seafood, including salmon, cod, halibut, and shellfish (such as clams, scallops and oysters). One particularly famous local clam is the geoduck.

Washington is famous for producing more than apples and clams, though. Nearly half of the state is covered in evergreen forests, and although it's not as essential as it once was, logging is still a big industry in Washington. Manufacturing is important to the state as well. The Boeing Company has been producing airplanes and airplane parts in the state for nearly a hundred years. Over the last two decades, Microsoft Corporation, based in Redmond, Washington, has become one of the most influential and innovative software manufacturers in the world.

Another popular industry in the state of Washington is the tourism industry. With national parks such as Olympic National Park, North Cascades National Park, and Mount Rainier National Park, and the active volcano Mount St. Helens in southwestern Washington, there are plenty of places to hike, boat, fish, hunt, and camp in the Evergreen State.

TRY THIS!

Apples!

More apples are grown in Washington State than in any other area in the world. In fact, the next time you go to the store, take a look at the apples that are displayed for sale. Wherever you live, there is a more than 90 percent chance that these apples will have a sticker that says "Grown in Washington"!

History

Before European exploration and settlement of the area, Washington was occupied by tribes who either spent most of their time on horseback or out in canoes fishing and hunting whales. The interior tribes such as the Yakama, Spokane, Palouse, Walla Walla, Colville, and Cayuse lived much as the Plains tribes did: moving from place to place and hunting buffalo nearly year-round. The coastal tribes, including the Duwamish, the Hoh, and the Makah, lived in long houses made from cedar planks, and hunted whales out on the open ocean in massive dugout canoes carved from the trunks of huge cedar trees.

During the sixteenth, seventeenth, and eighteenth centuries, Spanish sailors explored along Washington's coast, leaving their mark with place names such as the Strait of Juan de Fuca. In the late eighteenth century, Captain George Vancouver explored along Washington's coast looking for the mouth of the Columbia River (American sea captain Robert Gray had beaten him to it by just a few weeks).

The Only One

What makes the state of Washington's name unique?
To find out, fill in all the letters G and W, and the numbers 1 through 5.
Read the remaining white letters from left to right, and top to bottom!

WIGT1IGS23THGE3OWNGL
WY43SGTAWTGE5NWAGM
GE33D13AWFGT3EGR3WGA
2PGR3EGSGIGD2EGNT3!

American explorers Lewis and Clark visited the southern part of the state when they followed the Snake River out of Idaho and all the way to where it empties into the Columbia in 1805. After Lewis and Clark, the region was jointly occupied by citizens of the United States and Canadians (who were British subjects) for nearly forty years until the Oregon Treaty in 1846 split the region into the Canadian province of British Columbia and the American-run Oregon Territory.

When Oregon became a state in 1859, the rest of the territory became known as the Washington Territory. It included parts of what later became Idaho and Montana as well. In 1889, Washington became a state.

ALASKA: The Last Frontier

Geography and Industry

Alaska is beyond big, larger than large, more than massive. Alaska has so much land area in it that it would take 20 percent of the states that make up the forty-eight continental United States to equal the size of Alaska alone! When it comes to population, though, Alaska is on the other end of the spectrum. Only the states of Vermont and Wyoming have fewer people living within their borders.

Alaska is separated from the continental United States by western Canada, and is closer to Russian Siberia than to the rest of America. The northern part of the state is made up mostly of the Seward Peninsula, and lies above the Arctic Circle. This includes the North Slope, which is where most of Alaska's oil is produced. This region also contains Point Barrow.

The Yukon River runs out of the Yukon Territory in neighboring Canada, crosses Alaska from east to west, then empties into the Bering Sea, which borders Alaska on the west. Southwest of the Yukon River Valley lies the Alaska Peninsula, which stretches

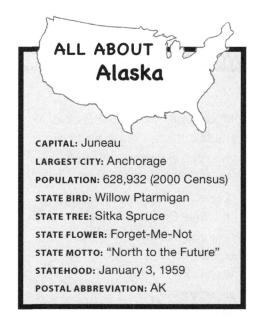

ALL ABOUT Alaska

CAPITAL: Juneau
LARGEST CITY: Anchorage
POPULATION: 628,932 (2000 Census)
STATE BIRD: Willow Ptarmigan
STATE TREE: Sitka Spruce
STATE FLOWER: Forget-Me-Not
STATE MOTTO: "North to the Future"
STATEHOOD: January 3, 1959
POSTAL ABBREVIATION: AK

Fun Facts

POINT BARROW

Point Barrow, which extends northward into the Arctic Ocean from Alaska's North Slope, is the northernmost point in the United States!

WORDS TO KNOW

Mount McKinley

Mount McKinley, which rises to a height of 20,320 feet, is the tallest mountain in America. Local Native American tribes called it "Denali," which means the Great One. (It is now commonly known by both names.) It was named for then-president William McKinley in 1897. The mountain sits at the center of Denali National Park.

out into the islands chain known as the Aleutians. These islands separate the Bering Sea from the northern Pacific, and are storm-ravaged, small, rocky, and barren. Few people live there these days.

Separating the Alaska Peninsula from the rest of southern Alaska is the massive Gulf of Alaska. The Kenai Peninsula pushes south of Anchorage (Alaska's largest city) and into the gulf in the direction of Kodiak Island.

Across the Gulf of Alaska from the Alaska Peninsula lies the so-called Alaskan Panhandle. It's made up mostly of small islands and a narrow coastal strip of land that rises quickly into the steep Coastal Range of mountains. The state capital of Juneau is in this region, which has a climate similar to that of western Washington state: lots of rain, not much snow (in Alaska, one of the snowiest states!).

To the north of Anchorage lies the Alaska Range of mountains, which are very snowy and very rugged. The Alaska Range's highest point is the summit of Mount McKinley.

Because it is so close to the fish-rich North Pacific, Alaska is home to a large year-round fishing fleet that catches millions of pounds of commercial fish per year. In 1968 oil was discovered on Alaska's North Slope, and petroleum extraction remains a very important industry in the state to this day. In fact, Alaska's oil reserves are the largest in North America. Alaska is also the only place in the United States where fur-trapping is still done to any noticeable extent.

History

Beginning in 1741 Russian fur traders explored much of southern Alaska, including the Aleutian Islands and the Alaskan Panhandle. They established their first permanent settlement on Kodiak Island in 1784.

Russia controlled Alaska for the next eighty years, and at various times tried to expand southward along the coast as far as Vancouver Island. In fact, in 1812 Russian settlers established a trading post in northern California at Fort Ross, near the Russian River (which they also named).

By the 1860s the Russian fur trade in Alaska had become so costly that there was no more profit to be made by continuing it, and the Russian Czar (king) sought to get something in return for it. He found a buyer in U.S. Secretary of State William Seward, who arranged for the United States to pay $7,200,000 for Alaska.

Big and Small

Alaska is one of the largest states while Rhode Island is one of the tiniest. Just how different in size are they? Figure out the following equations and you will learn how many times you could fit the state of Rhode Island into the state of Alaska!

The number of states:

MULTIPLY by the number of states with four letters in their name:

MULTIPLY by the number of states that start with the letter O:

SUBTRACT the total number of letters in Idaho, Missouri, Pennsylvania:

ANSWER:
The state of Rhode Island could fit into Alaska

_____ times!

125

Seward spent the rest of his career (and his life) defending this purchase. Alaska was known far and wide as either Seward's Icebox or Seward's Folly, because it seemed to be nothing more than an icy desert, virtually worthless.

Alaska did not even get a governor or official territorial government until after gold was discovered there in 1880. After that, things began to pick up, as other minerals were found and mined, including petroleum in 1968. Seward was proven to not just be right in the end, but to be brilliant, because Alaska has repaid its purchase price many times over since the United States acquired it. Alaska became the forty-ninth state in January of 1959.

PUERTO RICO

Geography and Industry

Puerto Rico isn't a state, but it's under the authority of the United States. Officially, it's a commonwealth, and its head of state (which in a state would be a governor) is the U.S. president. It does have a governor who is elected by Puerto Rico's voters.

Puerto Rico is an island in the eastern end of the West Indies. It is bordered on the south by the Caribbean Sea and on the north by the Atlantic Ocean. Located closer to the equator than the continental United States, the island is semitropical, with a long growing season and no discernable winter.

Puerto Rico is crossed by mountains such as the Cordillera Central. Its rivers are short and too shallow for river travel. The commonwealth of Puerto Rico includes several smaller off-shore islands, the largest of which is Vieques (VYA-kays).

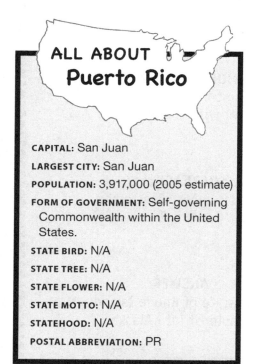

ALL ABOUT
Puerto Rico

CAPITAL: San Juan

LARGEST CITY: San Juan

POPULATION: 3,917,000 (2005 estimate)

FORM OF GOVERNMENT: Self-governing Commonwealth within the United States.

STATE BIRD: N/A

STATE TREE: N/A

STATE FLOWER: N/A

STATE MOTTO: N/A

STATEHOOD: N/A

POSTAL ABBREVIATION: PR

Puerto Rico's capital and largest city is San Juan. Other important cities include Caguas, Mayaguez, and Ponce.

Manufacturing of items such as clothing, electronics, and pharmaceuticals is Puerto Rico's main industry. Agriculture such as the raising of livestock, coffee, sugar cane, and tobacco are also very important to Puerto Rico's economy.

With its semitropical climate, lush scenery, and gorgeous white-sand beaches, Puerto Rico profits highly from year-round tourism. People from all over the world visit Puerto Rico for the beaches alone.

History

There were members of the Arawak tribe of native people living on Puerto Rico when Christopher Columbus visited it in 1493. In 1508, Juan Ponce de Leon led a force of conquistadors ashore on the island he named Puerto Rico (Spanish for "rich harbor") and conquered for Spain.

The Spaniards enslaved the local natives and forced them to work on the sugar plantations they built once they had conquered the island. As the Arawaks died out from overwork and disease, the Spaniards replaced them with black slaves brought from Africa.

Puerto Rico's capital city of San Juan quickly became a jewel in the crown of the Spanish Empire, with gorgeous buildings and a thriving economy. The rest of the island languished in a slow-moving sugar-based economic rut, which was made worse over the decades by repeated raids on the island by English, French, and Dutch buccaneers.

By the nineteenth century, Puerto Rico's native population had become dissatisfied with Spanish colonial rule, and there were several rebellions on the island. The Spanish brutally put down each one.

Fun Facts

PONCE DE LEON

Ponce de Leon conquered and named the island of Puerto Rico, and was the island's first governor. As a result of this expedition and his governorship, Ponce de Leon became a very wealthy man. And yet he isn't usually remembered for this accomplishment. He is remembered as the man who explored Florida looking for the Fountain of Youth and failed.

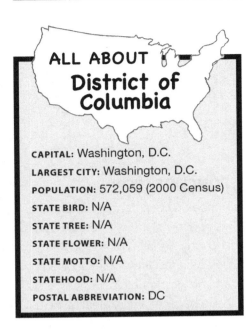

ALL ABOUT District of Columbia

CAPITAL: Washington, D.C.

LARGEST CITY: Washington, D.C.

POPULATION: 572,059 (2000 Census)

STATE BIRD: N/A

STATE TREE: N/A

STATE FLOWER: N/A

STATE MOTTO: N/A

STATEHOOD: N/A

POSTAL ABBREVIATION: DC

The situation changed in 1898, when the United States defeated Spain in the short and nearly bloodless Spanish-American War. As part of the treaty that ended the war, Spain ceded control of Puerto Rico to the United States.

In 1917 Puerto Ricans received both U.S. citizenship and the right to vote in their local elections. In the years since, they have had the choice to become independent, to stay a self-ruling commonwealth of the United States, or to become a state. The citizens of the island have chosen to remain a commonwealth.

THE DISTRICT OF COLUMBIA

Geography and Industry

This federal region on the Potomac River between the states of Maryland and Virginia is not a state. It is a district controlled directly by the U.S. Congress, and its sole purpose is to serve as the seat of the U.S. government in the form of the nation's capital: the city of Washington. It was once a ten-mile perfect square, and contained the village of Georgetown and the county of Alexandria, all situated on land donated by both Maryland and Virginia. The land on the Virginia side of the Potomac River was later given back to the state of Virginia.

The District of Columbia only has one industry: the U.S. government, which employs most of the people who live in the district. Others work for the city of Washington, which is another large employer within the district.

History

President George Washington chose the site of the United States' new capital city in 1790. French architect Pierre L'Enfant

won a contest with his plans for laying out the new city. It was designed on his proposed model.

At first the district was officially a territory, just like many of the states were before they became states. Unlike with other territories, though, the district was never intended to become a state, and has never had a governor. Until 1961 Americans who lived in the District of Columbia weren't even allowed to vote in presidential elections!

Slavery was abolished in the district in 1850 as a result of the political compromise of the same year (the Compromise of 1850, of course!). The territorial type of government was discontinued in 1874, and the president appointed a council to run the district's government. This lasted until 1967, when a mayor-council system was put in place. From 1967 until 1973, the president appointed the mayor and council members. In 1973, they became elected officials.

Fun Facts

THE SITE OF THE DISTRICT OF COLUMBIA

Located right on the Potomac River not far from George Washington's estate of Mount Vernon, the District of Columbia's location was personally selected by our first president. Many people since have wondered why he chose to build the nation's capital on what was at the time a swamp!

GLOSSARY: WEIRD WORDS

Adobe   A type of mud brick used to build huge apartment houses in the American Southwest before the arrival of the Europeans.

Badlands   An area of wind-sculpted rock formations and arid climate in western North Dakota.

Black Hills   A collection of low mountains that rise right off of the floor of the Great Plains. Considered sacred by the Sioux Indians.

Buckeye   Both Ohio's state tree and the mascot of the Ohio State University.

Cahokia   A large pre-Columbian Native American settlement that at one time was home to almost 40,000 people.

Cajun   French-Canadian refugees and their descendants, and the culture they've developed in Louisiana's swamp area.

Confederacy   A political unit that consists of smaller groups coming together to form a larger, not very cohesive group (differing from a "union," which is a tighter-knit grouping).

Conifer   A type of tree that has needles for leaves and drops cones in order to reproduce, rather than dropping seeds as deciduous trees do.

Continental Divide   The crest of the Rocky Mountains and the spine of the continent. On the east side of this divide, all water runs east, into the Atlantic; on the west side, all water runs west, into the Pacific.

Croatoan   A mysterious Native American word found carved on a doorpost of a house in the empty "lost colony" of Roanoke, North Carolina.

DelMarVa Peninsula   A peninsula that separates Chesapeake Bay from the Atlantic Ocean, and takes its name from the abbreviations for the three states that occupy parts of it: Delaware, Maryland, and Virginia.

Delta   A triangular piece of land made up of deposited river silt, and always found at the mouth of a river.

Fundamental Orders   Connecticut's first set of colonial governing rules.

Geoduck   A rare species of giant clam found only in and around Washington state's Puget Sound.

Hessians   Soldiers from Germany hired by King George III of England to fight against the rebels during the American Revolution.

Glossary

Humuhumunukunukuapuaa The Hawaiian state fish. We call them triggerfish.

Iroquois A powerful Native American confederation of several tribes in Western New York. Called themselves "Ho-de-no-sau-nee."

Kan-Tuck-Kee An Algonquian phrase that means "Dark and Bloody Ground." The modern state of Kentucky gets its name from this phrase.

Lake Chargoggmaunchaugagoggchaubungungamaugg A small lake (more like a pond) in Massachusetts whose name comes from the agreement two tribes of Native Americans came to about the use of it: "You fish on your side of the lake and I'll fish on my side of the lake, and nobody fishes in the middle."

Louisiana Purchase The largest land sale in recorded history, where France sold all of its remaining New World possessions to the United States.

Mesa Spanish for "table." It refers to the type of rocky butte that in this case has a very flat top. Found mostly in the desert southwest.

Moraine Any boulders, trees, rocks, soil, or other material left behind by a retreating glacier.

Mormon Member of the Church of Jesus Christ of Latter-Day Saints, or referring to something about this church.

Muskogean A language family among the Native American tribes who lived all over the South.

Nomad A person or a group of persons who do not settle down and stay in one place. Rather, they travel all over, hunting herd animals, and so on.

Opechancanough Pocahontas's uncle, who fought the settlers at Jamestown.

Over-fishing What happens when fishermen catch too many of a type of fish, not leaving enough to replenish themselves. It leads to extinction of those fish.

Panhandle A nickname for a narrow section of a state or country that juts out away from the rest of the state.

Pequot A tribe of Native Americans who fought a disastrous and bloody war with English colonists in New England during the seventeenth century.

Piedmont A collection of rolling hills, usually fertile, and usually lying as transitional ground between coastal lowlands and higher elevations.

Powhatan The title (like "chief" or "king") used by Pocahontas's father, who ruled the Powhatan confederation.

  131

Pueblo   Referring both to the mud-brick cities of the farmers of the early southwest and to the tribes themselves.

Puritan   A member of the Church of England who wanted to reform, or "purify," the church.

Rural   Describes a place that is not in a city or suburb, that is still wild, with few roads or houses. A country setting.

Secession   When one part of a country or state attempts to leave that country or state.

Sooner   A nickname for a resident of Oklahoma that refers to filing a land claim "sooner" than his competitors.

Stalactite   An icicle-shaped piece of rock that hangs from cave ceilings.

Stalagmite   Like a stalactite, except that it thrusts up from the floor of the cavern.

Suffrage   The right to vote in an election.

Tejas   Spanish word for "friends." We get the name for our state of Texas from this word. Actually, it's the Spanish spelling of a Caddo word taysha, which means "friend" or "ally."

Tornado   A weather phenomenon that causes winds to blow in tighter and tighter circles.

Unicameral   Comes from the Latin word meaning "one house." In this case, it refers to the fact that Nebraska's state government only has one house of government, not two (such as a house of representatives and a senate) like most states do.

Yellowhammer   Alabama's state bird.

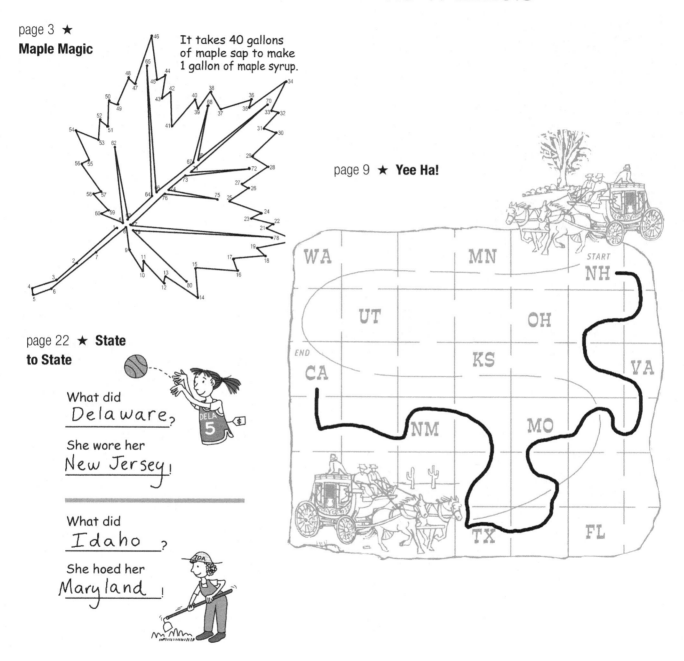

page 3 ★
Maple Magic

It takes 40 gallons
of maple sap to make
1 gallon of maple syrup.

page 9 ★ **Yee Ha!**

page 22 ★ **State
to State**

What did
Delaware?

She wore her
New Jersey!

What did
Idaho?

She hoed her
Maryland!

page 31 ★ **One to Grow On**

HAPPY BIRTH-
DAY ||||
TO YOU

page 41 ★ **Pickles?**

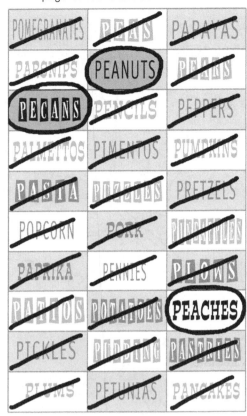

POMEGRANATES · PEAS · PAPAYAS
PARSNIPS · (PEANUTS) · PEARS
(PECANS) · PENCILS · PEPPERS
PALMETTOS · PIMENTOS · PUMPKINS
PASTA · PUZZLES · PRETZELS
POPCORN · PORK · POTATOES
PAPRIKA · PENNIES · PLOWS
PATIOS · POTATOES · (PEACHES)
PICKLES · PUDDING · PASTRIES
PLUMS · PETUNIAS · PANCAKES

page 46 ★ **Where are my glasses?**

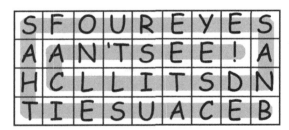

S	F	O	U	R	E	Y	E	S
A	A	N	'	T	S	E	E	!	A
H	C	L	L	I	T	S	D	N
T	I	E	S	U	A	C	E	B

**Because it has four
eyes and still can't see!**
(I's)

page 51 ★ **Get in Shape**

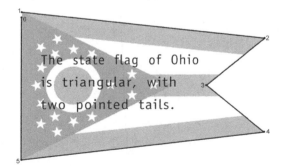

The state flag of Ohio
is triangular, with
two pointed tails.

Puzzle Answers

page 54 ★ Crossing Indiana

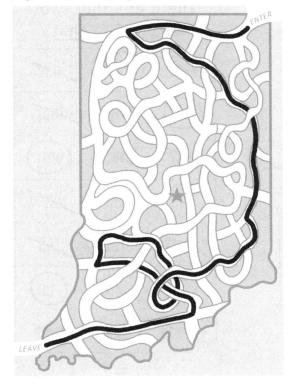

page 67 ★ Rock 'n' Roll

W 23rd	H F+2	A 1st	T R+2		S 19th	O before P	U 21st	T S+1	H J-2
D A+3	A E-4	K L-1	O after N	T V-2	A Z-25	N 14th			
R 18th	O M+2	C 3rd	K J+1		G F+1	R S-1	O Q-2	U T+1	P 16th
H 8th	A 1st	S 19th		F D+2	O M+2	U 21st	R P+2		
M L+1	E 5th	N 14th		W Z-3	H 8th	O Q-2			
D 4th	O M+2	N P-2	' T 20th		S 19th	I G+2	N 14th	G I-2	?
M after L	O Q-2	U V-1	N M+1	T 20th					
R Q+1	U 21st	S before T	H 8th	M before N	O N+1	R after Q	E 5th	!	

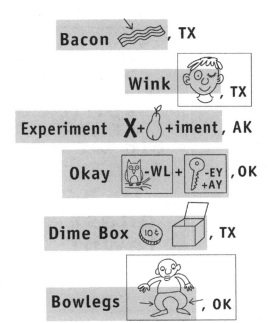

Bacon 〰〰, TX

Wink 😉, TX

Experiment X + 🍐 +iment, AK

Okay 🦉-WL + 🔑-EY+AY, OK

Dime Box 🪙 📦, TX

page 76 ★ You Live Where?

Bowlegs 🧍, OK

page 83 ★ **Life in LA**

The

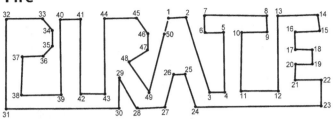

Jean Lafitte had a hideaway in Louisiana.

The brown

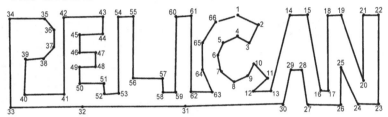

is the Louisiana state bird.

page 119 ★ **Scared Silly**

There are only two
letters T in <u>that</u>!

~~twelve~~	(there)	~~lone~~
(are)	~~simply~~	~~four~~
~~more~~	~~thirteen~~	(only)
(two)	~~star~~	~~thirty~~
~~plenty~~	(letters)	~~ten~~
(T)	~~store~~	(in)
~~twenty~~	(that)	~~state~~

page 122 ★ **The Only One**

It is the only state
named after a president!

WIGT1IGS23THGE3OWNGL
WY43SGTAWTGE5NWAGM
GE33D13AWFGT3EGR3WGA
2PGR3EGSGIGD2EGNT3!

The number of states:

50

MULTIPLY by the
number of states with
four letters in their name:

3 *Utah, Ohio, Iowa*

MULTIPLY by
number of states that
start with the letter O:

3 *Oregon, Oklahoma, Ohio*

SUBTRACT the
total number of letters in
Idaho, Missouri, Pennsylvania:

25

ANSWER:
The state of Rhode Island
could fit into Alaska

425 times!

page 125 ★ **Big and Small**

Made in the USA
Middletown, DE
17 March 2020